This poster was printed in the late 1930s to advertise swimming lessons given by the New York Department of Parks. Eve[...] the lessons were open to all children, the design suggests that white children would be taught separately from black chi[...]

MILES TO GO FOR FREEDOM

SEGREGATION & CIVIL RIGHTS IN THE JIM CROW YEARS

Linda Barrett Osborne

Published in association with

THE LIBRARY OF CONGRESS

ABRAMS BOOKS FOR YOUNG READERS · NEW YORK

To teachers and librarians, who pass on the legacy of American history to their students, so that they can better understand the past and shape a better future

Library of Congress Cataloging-in-Publication Data

Osborne, Linda Barrett, 1949–
Miles to go for freedom : segregation and civil rights in the Jim Crow years / by Linda Barrett Osborne.
p. cm.
"Published in association with the Library of Congress."
Includes bibliographical references and index.
ISBN 978-1-4197-0020-0
1. African Americans—Segregation—History—20th century—Juvenile literature. 2. African Americans—Civil rights—
History—20th century—Juvenile literature. 3. Civil rights movements—United States—History—20th century—
Juvenile literature. 4. United States—Race relations—Juvenile literature. I. Library of Congress. II. Title.
E185.61.O827 2011
305.896'073009041—dc23
2011022854

Copyright © 2012 Library of Congress
Book design by Maria T. Middleton

For image credits, please see page 114.

Excerpt on page 62 from **"Get Back (Black, Brown and White),"** words and music by William Lee Conley Broonzy © 1952
(renewed 1980) SCREEN GEMS-EMI MUSIC INC. All rights reserved. International copyright secured. Used by permission.
Reprinted by permission of Hal Leonard Corporation.

Printed and bound in China
10 9 8 7 6 5 4 3 2 1

Abrams Books for Young Readers are available at special discounts when purchased in quantity for premiums and
promotions as well as fundraising or educational use. Special editions can also be created to specification. For details,
contact specialsales@abramsbooks.com or the address below.

ABRAMS
THE ART OF BOOKS SINCE 1949
115 West 18th Street
New York, NY 10011
www.abramsbooks.com

CONTENTS

These African American children, posed on a porch in Georgia, were photographed in 1899 or 1900, just three or four years after the Supreme Court decision *Plessy v. Ferguson* declared that separating black and white people traveling on trains was legal. The children would grow up under a system of segregation that affected all aspects of their lives.

PREFACE

"At fifteen, I was fully conscious of the racial difference, and while I was sullen and resentful in my soul, I was beaten and knew it," remembered Albon Holsey. He was an African American teenager in the early 1900s, growing up in the South. "I knew then that I could never aspire to be President of the United States, nor Governor of my State, nor mayor of my city; I knew that the front doors of white homes in my town were not for me to enter, except as a servant; I knew that I could only sit in the peanut gallery [balcony] at our theatre, and could only ride on the back seat of the electric car."

We've come a long way since Albon Holsey reflected on his future at the turn of the twentieth century. In the 1960s, African Americans began to be elected as mayor of cities both large and small. (There had been black mayors from the 1860s until the 1880s, before most black men lost the vote.) Carl Stokes was the first African American elected mayor of a big city, Cleveland, Ohio, in 1967. In 1989, Douglas Wilder was the first African American elected governor of a state, Virginia; and in 2006, Deval Patrick became the second black American to be elected governor, this time of Massachusetts. In 2008, Barack Obama became the first African American to be elected president of the United States.

But what was life like for Holsey and millions of other black Americans before the 1960s? In the South, they lived under a system of legal segregation, informally called "Jim Crow," which defined and restricted their activities, their behavior, and their opportunities. Although many people believed that this had always been the southern way of life, African Americans had enjoyed some civil rights and a measure of freedom from the end of the Civil War in 1865 through the early 1890s. How and why did they lose this freedom? What was the impact of segregation on day-to-day life for black Americans, particularly for a young person? Did Jim Crow operate outside the South, in the northern, midwestern, and western states? How did federal policy affect segregation on a national level? How did African Americans fight back to regain their civil rights in the first half of the twentieth century?

This book considers these questions, focusing on the period between 1896, when the Supreme Court decision in *Plessy v. Ferguson* condoned—that is, approved or found acceptable—the notion of "separate but equal" public accommodations, and 1954, when it declared in *Brown v. Board of Education* that segregated schools could never be equal because their very existence as separate proclaimed that one race was better than another. *Miles to Go for Freedom* is a companion to my book *Traveling the Freedom Road: From Slavery and the Civil War Through Reconstruction*, which explores U.S. history and the lives of young black Americans from 1800 through 1877. This volume stops short of the protests and marches of the classic civil rights movement of the mid- to late-1950s and 1960s, which is covered by a large number of fine books for both children and adults.

For as long as African Americans have been oppressed, they have struggled for their civil rights. Many of the images and personal remembrances in this book capture the experiences of children and teenagers as they encountered—and tried to overcome— racism. Knowing how segregation developed and what it was like to live under that system links the nineteenth and twentieth centuries with the present in ways that illuminate both. This book cannot cover every topic and event of the Jim Crow years. But by broadening the scope to include Jim Crow as it was practiced not only in the South but in the rest of the nation, as well as by the federal government, it presents an overview of how African Americans lived in all parts of our country. It is not enough, however, to describe segregation and discrimination; it is equally important that Americans understand how African Americans resisted efforts to control and limit their lives, not just during the 1950s and 1960s but also as a continuous part of their history. A knowledge of these efforts and experiences is essential to understanding the civil rights movement that ended legal segregation; it is also key to understanding U.S. racial history, which still affects attitudes, policies, and politics today.

The words "race" and "racial" are used in this book as they were used both legally and informally in the period it covers. These words connote a difference between people descended from Africans and those descended from Europeans—blacks and whites. (Asians and other ethnic groups were thought to be of different races from European Americans, but I mention them only briefly.) "Race" was part of the language of the time. The Fifteenth Amendment to the U.S. Constitution says that the right to vote shall not be denied "on account of race." The Supreme Court decision in *Plessy v. Ferguson* is "founded in the color of the two races . . . which must always exist so long as white men are distinguished from the other race by color." The Supreme Court that issued the decision in *Brown v. Board of Education* considered "segregation of children in public schools solely on the basis of race." The courts, legislators, and ordinary people who used these words assumed there was a difference—biologically, intellectually, culturally—between persons descended from different ethnic backgrounds; they accepted these differences based on the perceived difference in physical traits. Race and color were bound together. Yet light-skinned individuals could be considered black because of their self-identification with African ancestry or the way in which their communities perceived them.

If anything, however, researching and writing about the Jim Crow period may be the best antidote to accepting any concept of race. Personal stories, political debates, court decisions, and academic writing all show how subjective and arbitrary a concept it is. In *Miles to Go for Freedom*, I use the word to record a time in our history, and "race"—what it meant or didn't mean, what it could promise or deny—is a central part of this history. But I am grateful for every effort that moves us beyond race, that takes us beyond insufficient and misleading categories, that helps us to welcome and celebrate the diversity of our human community.

African American boy drinks at a water fountain labeled "colored" in Halifax, North Carolina, in 1938. By the 1930s, segregation was well established in the southern states. This photograph was taken by John Vachon, who worked on a special project for the federal government to make a record of the way people lived across the United States.

INTRODUCTION

"I remember this little place near the bus station that sold the best hot dogs I ever ate," said Charles Epps, who was a child in the 1940s in Windsor, North Carolina. "If you were a white person, you could just go in, sit down, and enjoy your hot dog. But if you were black, you had to go around back. There was a little hole, about twelve inches by twelve inches, and you put your money through the opening. Then they would pass you a hot dog through the hole."

Charles Epps grew up in a time when many Americans lived under segregation. Black people and white people were segregated (separated) in schools, restaurants, movie theaters, and hotels, on trains and buses—almost any place where they might meet. In the eleven southern states that formed the Confederate States of America and fought against the Union in the Civil War (1861–65), segregation was a system of laws passed starting in the 1890s and valid until the 1960s. These states, often referred to as "the South," were Alabama, Arkansas, Florida, Georgia, Louisiana, Mississippi, North Carolina, South Carolina, Tennessee, Texas, and Virginia. In addition, a large number of laws that separated black and white people were passed in several states that bordered the South: Delaware, Kentucky, Maryland, Missouri, Oklahoma, and West Virginia.

Some states had laws that separated black and white Americans. Others passed laws against discrimination. This map shows the situation in 1949: states where laws segregated white people from people of color; states with anti-discrimination laws (although discrimination still happened in those states); and states with no laws about segregation or discrimination.

SEGREGATION ENFORCED BY LAW
DISCRIMINATION PROHIBITED BY LAW
NO LEGISLATION

In 1940, signs marked "white" and "colored" showed patrons where to enter this Durham, North Carolina, café. City codes in the South separated African Americans and whites at restaurants. In some places, black people could eat in a different section; in some, they could buy food but had to eat it outside; and in other places, they could not enter at all. This photograph was taken by Jack Delano.

Although many people think that segregation operated only in the South, the northern, midwestern, and western states (collectively called "the North" in this book) also passed laws that segregated people; one-fifth of all segregation laws came from these states. The majority of these laws segregated African Americans, but there were also laws that segregated Asians and American Indians from white people. Many called for segregated schools or made marriage between a white and a person of color illegal.

Even where there were no laws in the North, blacks suffered from discrimination. They were denied access to the same housing, jobs, and education as whites and were treated as second-class citizens. In the South, in addition to laws, customs and unspoken rules decided how blacks and whites ought to behave. Charles Gratton, a black man who grew up near Birmingham, Alabama, in the 1930s, said, "I can remember . . . when my mother would send me to this grocery store that was approximately a mile away. . . . She would give me instructions before I'd leave home and tell me, 'Son, now you go on up to [the] store and get this or that for me. If you pass any white people on your way, you get off the sidewalk. Give them the sidewalk. You move over. Don't challenge white people.'" Segregation not only separated blacks and whites in daily life; custom demanded that African Americans act at all times as if they were inferior to white people.

States passed segregation laws; so did cities and towns. The Birmingham, Alabama, city code in 1944 stated, "It shall be unlawful to conduct a restaurant or other places for the serving of food . . . at which white and colored people are served in the same room, unless such white and colored persons are effectively separated by a solid partition extending from the floor upward to a distance of seven feet or higher." The Durham, North Carolina, code of 1947 also required blacks and whites to eat in separate rooms: "The partition between such rooms shall be constructed [of] wood, plaster or brick . . . and shall reach from the floor to the ceiling." Anyone who didn't follow this rule could be arrested and, if convicted, would have to "pay a fine of ten dollars."

A Georgia law stated, "It shall be unlawful for any amateur white baseball team to play baseball on any vacant lot or baseball diamond within two blocks of a playground devoted to the Negro race, and it shall be unlawful for any amateur colored baseball team to play baseball in any vacant lot or baseball diamond within two blocks of any playground devoted to the white race." Birmingham in 1944 also made it "unlawful for a Negro and a white person to play together . . . in any game of cards, dice, dominoes, checkers, baseball, softball, football, basketball or similar games." Imagine any way to keep black and white people apart, and it seems there was a law that covered the situation.

Many Americans believed that segregation had started after the Civil War or went further back into the days of slavery. "From the time I grew up, you had white folks and black folks. And basically the black folks worked for the white folks. They . . . lived in their part of town and we lived in our part of town," said Leonard Barrow Jr., a white man, about his childhood in New Iberia, Louisiana, in the 1920s. "I guess if you didn't grow up here it would be difficult to understand, it was two separate worlds. You know, you just didn't become part of their world, you didn't go into their houses, they worked in your house, but it was just the way it was. It had always been that way."

But it hadn't *always* been that way, although the ideas that black and white Americans had about each other did have their roots in slavery. Slaves in the United States were Africans or descended from Africans. By the time of the Civil War, the great majority of slaves had been born in the United States.

Segregation laws called for separate parks for black and white people. This 1945 photograph shows African American boys diving into Jones Lake in North Carolina, in the park set aside for blacks.

They worked not for wages but for their owners' profit. They had no freedom to change jobs or the place where they lived. They had no political rights. They were usually forbidden to learn to read and write. Slaves could be beaten and even killed by their owners or other white people. Many whites who defended slavery believed that African Americans were inferior to white people and saw no reason to treat them with respect.

By the early 1800s, northern states had abolished slavery, but it thrived in the South. Americans argued over whether slavery should be legal anywhere. The eleven states that formed the Confederate States of America in 1861 fought the Civil War against the Union (the rest of the United States) in large part to preserve slavery. But the Confederate States lost the Civil War in 1865, and that same year the Thirteenth Amendment to the U.S. Constitution freed the slaves. The U.S. Congress took several steps to help these freedmen and freedwomen. In 1865 it created the Bureau of Refugees, Freedmen, and Abandoned Lands— known as the Freedmen's Bureau—to aid them in reuniting with family

THE RESULT OF THE FIFTEENTH AMENDMENT,
And the Rise and Progress of the African Race in America and its final Accomplishment, and Celebration on May 19th A.D. 1870.
BALTIMORE, PUBLISHED BY METCALF & CLARK, 537 W. BALTIMORE ST.

The Fifteenth Amendment to the U.S. Constitution says that neither a state nor the nation can deny African American men the right to vote. The center of this lithograph shows a celebration by black people in Baltimore, Maryland, soon after the amendment was adopted, in March 1870. Around the border are portraits of men who fought or helped to end slavery and scenes of a black schoolroom and church.

members separated by slave owners, getting an education, and finding jobs in a fair system of employment. Many freedmen left the places where they had been slaves, and most chose to work for wages or to sharecrop—to farm a piece of land owned by someone else in return for a share of the crop at harvest.

By the end of 1865, however, the cities and states in the South had begun to create laws that governed how the freedmen had to behave and on what terms they could work. Taken together, these laws were known as Black Codes. For example, some laws didn't allow blacks to travel at night without a pass from their employer or forbade them from having friends to visit. Others restricted the kinds of jobs African Americans could have. Black Codes re-created as much as possible the system of slavery; they were the first of many attempts by the South to control how African Americans lived and worked for the next hundred years.

Congress responded to these Black Codes by passing a law to protect the civil rights of freedmen in 1866. In 1868, the Fourteenth Amendment became part of the U.S. Constitution, guaranteeing African Americans citizenship and stating that they should be treated fairly and in the same way as white people under the law. The Fifteenth Amendment, adopted in 1870, granted black men the right to vote. (Women of any race could not vote in national elections until 1920.) For the next two decades, disfranchisement (not being allowed to vote) and rigid legal segregation did not exist. African Americans could serve on juries and hold local, state, or national office. While serving in state legislatures and in the U.S. Congress, they passed laws to improve education and to ensure that black people could ride on public transportation and go to public places like theaters and hotels, using the same accommodations as white people did. African Americans gained these rights and opportunities during the period

In early 1867, Congress passed a bill allowing black men in the District of Columbia to vote. President Andrew Johnson vetoed it, but Congress overruled him. The magazine *Harper's Weekly* printed this wood engraving of African American men voting for the first time in the nation's capital in 1867. The Fifteenth Amendment, passed in 1870, gave all black men the right to vote.

known as Reconstruction, when the South was rebuilt after the damage to its land and people caused by the Civil War.

Frequently, however, some southern whites prevented African Americans from exercising their political and civil rights through intimidation and violence. They formed organizations like the Ku Klux Klan to terrorize blacks who expressed independence, acquired land and wealth, or voted. Black people could lose their jobs, their homes, and even their lives. Their best protection came from the U.S. government. The Freedmen's Bureau and U.S. (federal) soldiers stationed in the South after the Civil War tried to limit the violence and supported the former slaves in exercising their rights. But the Freedmen's Bureau was disbanded in 1872, and the last federal troops were withdrawn in 1877, which is considered the year that Reconstruction ended. For decades to come, the national government stepped back from its involvement with rights and politics in the South.

The South did not immediately start passing segregation laws when Reconstruction ended. Many whites still felt that they were better than African Americans; many still tried to control how, when, and where they worked. Black people suffered discrimination in schools, housing, transportation, and jobs. But for more than twenty years, southern blacks continued to exercise some freedoms. They rode on integrated trains and streetcars. They were elected to state legislatures—in North Carolina, fifty-two African Americans were elected between 1876 and 1894; and in South Carolina, forty-seven were elected between 1878 and 1902. Between 1869 and 1901, with the exception of one year, at least one African American served in the U.S. Congress. Blacks were appointed to offices at the county and local level.

Pauli Murray, a civil rights activist and lawyer, recalled how her African American family lived in North Carolina after Reconstruction. "Uncle Richard Fitzgerald was known as the town's leading brick manufacturer and was considered wealthy," she wrote. "He owned a great deal of property all over town and was president of the first Negro bank organized in Durham. He and his family lived in a fine eighteen-room slate-roofed house. . . . When my aunts went to town, men of good breeding tipped their hats. . . . They went where they pleased . . . and were all grown women before the first law requiring separation on trains and streetcars appeared in North Carolina."

This elegant and well-dressed black woman was photographed in 1899 or 1900. At the end of the nineteenth century, African Americans in the South still had some rights and opportunities to prosper, especially depending on where they lived. However, once the rigid rules and laws of segregation were established, life became much more difficult for all classes of blacks—poor

Black men like Pauli Murray's uncle continued to vote after 1877, and white candidates went after their support. The Republican Party had promoted civil rights in the 1860s and 1870s, championing black as well as white candidates, and traditionally claimed black loyalty. In the 1890s, some members of the Populist Party, a largely white group of farmers and workingmen who sought better working and economic conditions, formed alliances with black people to improve opportunities for everyone. Even some former Confederate leaders courted blacks to gain their votes, offering promises of fewer race-based laws and a few government jobs in return. As long as political candidates saw African Americans as a group that could influence elections, blacks had some political power.

Whites could limit this power by using threats and violence, but they could not completely silence it. In the 1880s, more than two-thirds of all black men in the South voted. Whites who believed that African Americans were inferior, who wanted to control how and where blacks could work, and who thought that only white people should take part in government were angry and determined to make a change. They were especially concerned in those states that had a larger black population than white population. The 1890 census showed more African Americans than whites living in Louisiana, Mississippi, and South Carolina, and almost an equal number of blacks and whites in Alabama and Georgia.

The Fifteenth Amendment said that a man could not be denied the right to vote because of race, color, or previous condition of servitude (having been a slave). The southern states had to find a reason that black men could be denied this right. The first to try was Mississippi, and it used the method all the states of the former Confederacy would come to use: rewriting its state constitution.

Mississippi's new state constitution of 1890 said that if a person wanted to register to vote, he had to be able to pass a literacy test to prove he could read and write, which some blacks as well as whites could not. Voters also had to pay a tax to be able to vote (a poll tax). Since many African Americans lived in poverty, they could not afford to pay the tax. Nor could poor whites, and in fact, some white men did lose the vote under Mississippi's new constitution because they were poor or couldn't read.

In 1895, South Carolina changed its state constitution to limit voting in various ways, as did Louisiana in 1898. Although the Mississippi voting rules had been challenged in the Supreme Court, in 1898 the court ruled that literacy tests and poll taxes did not violate the Fifteenth Amendment (in *Williams v. Mississippi*). In quick order came changes to the constitutions of North Carolina (1900), Alabama (1901), Virginia (1902), and Georgia (1908). Arkansas, Florida, Tennessee, and Texas instituted the poll tax to exclude voters. By the early 1900s, two out of every three southern men (including white men) could not vote. The Supreme Court's 1898 decision made it possible to effectively deny African Americans the right to vote for nearly seventy years—until the U.S. Congress passed, and President Lyndon Johnson signed, the Voting Rights Act in 1965.

Congressman George H. White, the last black member of the U.S. House of Representatives in the nineteenth century, understood that African Americans were being denied the vote, not because they had failed to prosper after the Civil War but because some of them were succeeding. "We seem as a race to be going through just now . . . a crisis," he said in 1899. "Possibly more than by any one thing it has been brought about by the fact that despite all the oppression which has fallen upon our shoulders we have been rising, steadily

HEROES OF THE COLORED RACE.

Black men served in state legislatures and the U.S. Congress until 1901. This print, published in 1881, shows two African American senators: Blanche Kelso Bruce (*left*) and Hiram Rhoades Revels (*right*). Frederick Douglass, an escaped slave, a famous abolitionist, and an advocate for civil rights, is in the center. The border depicts scenes of African American life and portraits of people who supported black freedom

rising, and in some instances we hope ere [before] long to be able to measure our achievements with those of all other men and women of the land. This tendency on the part of some of us to rise and assert our manhood . . . is, I fear, what has brought about this changed condition."

Without the vote, African Americans could not protect their other rights. They had no way of stopping lawmakers who believed that whites were superior to blacks. They had no power to prevent state governments from passing laws that separated white and black people. Segregation laws began to spring up in the South and the border states in the 1890s—the same decade that black men were denied the vote.

Black and white picnickers are clearly separated at this barbecue, given every year by F. M. Gay in Alabama. Why they have gathered in this fashion is unknown. The photograph was taken sometime between 1930 and 1941.

THE SOUTH

On June 7, 1892, Homer Plessy boarded a train in New Orleans that was bound for Covington, Louisiana, sixty miles away. Plessy was a shoemaker who worked in the city. His skin was light—he had white as well as black ancestors. Could he ride in a train car set aside for white passengers?

In 1890, the state of Louisiana had passed a law requiring train companies to provide separate cars for white and black passengers and to ensure that each car remain segregated. This was unusual—since the end of the Civil War, blacks and whites had traveled together in trains. African Americans had also served in the state governments. In fact, when the Louisiana General Assembly passed this law, sixteen African Americans were members of the legislature, although they could not stop the white majority from voting to segregate the trains. Under this new law, passengers could be fined twenty-five dollars or be jailed for twenty days if they sat in the "wrong" car. A railroad employee could also be fined or jailed if he gave a seat to a black passenger in a white car.

Homer Plessy belonged to the Citizens' Committee to Test the Constitutionality of the Separate Car Law. The group told the railroad company beforehand what Plessy was going to do. He was testing the law—he knowingly sat in a railroad car set aside for whites, expecting that he would not be allowed

to keep his seat. When the conductor asked him whether he was a white man, Plessy "replied that he was a colored man," even though he looked white. He was considered to be a "colored" man in Louisiana and the other southern states because some of his ancestors were black. The conductor then asked Plessy to move to a car for blacks, and he refused. He never finished the trip to Covington; he was promptly arrested, taken off the train, and put in jail.

Plessy did not mind being arrested. He carried out his plan to challenge in the local court the train segregation law under which he had been jailed. His lawyer argued that it went against the U.S. Constitution's Thirteenth Amendment (abolishing slavery) and Fourteenth Amendment (granting equal protection under the law) and was therefore not valid. The charges should be dismissed. Judge John Ferguson ruled that this was incorrect—he said the law was not unconstitutional. Plessy's case then went to the Louisiana Supreme Court and on to the Supreme Court of the United States.

The all-white, all-male U.S. Supreme Court heard Plessy's case on May 18, 1896. Seven of the eight judges who heard the case decided against him. (One judge, David Brewer, did not hear the case or take part in the decision.) The seven judges said that the Louisiana law was not unconstitutional—it was not illegal to provide separate train cars for whites and blacks as long as those train cars were equal. Even though the phrase "separate but equal" was not written in the judges' decision, this ruling became known as the "separate but equal" doctrine. It was used to justify legal segregation for more than fifty years. In support of separation, Justice Henry Billings Brown stated that there would always be a difference between black and white Americans "founded in the color of the two races . . . which . . . must always exist so long as white men are distinguished from the other race by color."

Justices of the
United States Supreme Court.

The nine white, male judges of the U.S. Supreme Court in 1896 are pictured here. Chief Justice Melville Fuller is in the center. Clockwise from top right: Horace Gray, Rufus W. Peckham, Edward D. White, John M. Harlan, Henry B. Brown, David J. Brewer, Stephen J. Field, and George Shiras Jr. The Court decided in *Plessy v. Ferguson* that separate facilities for black people did not violate the Constitution if the facilities were equal. Justice Harlan was the only judge to disagree.

The decision also said that it was a mistake to think that "the enforced separation of the two races stamps the colored race with a badge of inferiority." Schools had long been segregated in many states, and no court had declared that illegal. But schools were a perfect example of inequality under segregation: white students went to school in better buildings, with better books and equipment, than black students. In practice, the separate facilities for African Americans were always inferior to those for whites and would remain so. Even if the facilities had been equal, the *Plessy* decision was saying that blacks and whites were from distinct and different races, instead of from the same *human race*.

Justice John Marshall Harlan was the only Supreme Court judge in 1896 to disagree with this decision. He wrote, "The constitution of the United States does not, I think, permit any public authority to know the race of those entitled to be protected in the enjoyment of [their civil] rights." Harlan also wrote that "the common government of all shall not permit the seeds of race hate to be planted under the sanction of law. What can more certainly arouse race hate . . . than state enactments which . . . proceed on the ground that colored citizens are so inferior and degraded that they cannot be allowed to sit in public coaches occupied by white citizens."

The other judges in *Plessy v. Ferguson* said that it was foolish to think that allowing segregation in train cars would lead to other kinds of segregation—that there would be "separate cars . . . provided for people whose hair is of a certain color, or who are aliens, or who belong to certain nationalities." Nor, they stated, would states begin to "enact laws requiring colored people to walk upon one side of the street, and white people upon the other; or requiring white men's houses to be painted white, and colored men's black."

But a system very much like that did, in fact, come about.

By 1900, laws in almost every southern state required black and white Americans to ride in separate train cars. South Carolina passed such a law in 1898, and North Carolina passed one a year later. Until 1900, Georgia was the only state that required blacks and whites to be segregated on streetcars as well as trains. Then North Carolina and Virginia called for streetcar segregation in 1901; Louisiana in 1902; Arkansas, South Carolina, and Tennessee in 1903; Mississippi in 1904; and Florida in 1905. The border states of Maryland and Oklahoma mandated streetcar segregation in 1904 and 1907, respectively.

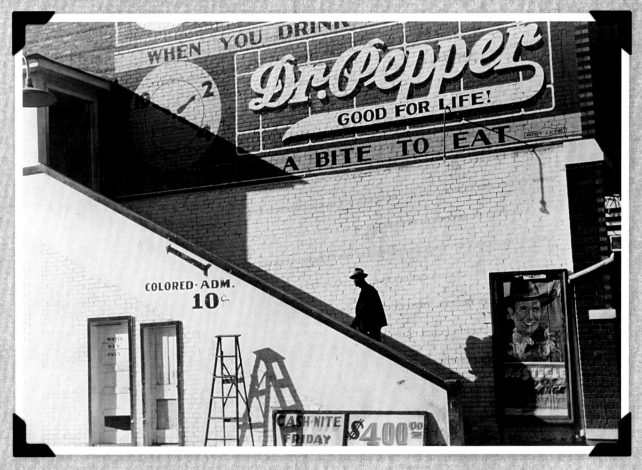

In the years following 1900, state segregation laws and local regulations became numerous. They kept African Americans out of whites-only schools, restaurants, hotels, movie theaters, bus and train station waiting rooms, libraries, hospitals, and other public facilities. They also covered very specific actions and situations. A 1905 law in Georgia declared that anyone could donate land to a city for a park, but the donor had to state whether the park would be for white people only or black people only. In Mobile, Alabama, a 1909 law required African Americans to be off the streets by ten p.m.

After 1900, hundreds of laws and codes required segregation in the South. This 1939 photo shows an African American man climbing to the "colored" entrance of a movie theater in Belzoni, Mississippi. Black people had to sit in the balcony at segregated theaters, while white people sat on the ground floor. A bathroom marked "white men only" is at the lower left of this photograph, taken by Marion Post Wolcott.

RIGHT A crowd waiting for a bus at the terminal in Memphis, Tennessee, stands below a sign indicating the "white waiting room." The passengers also will be segregated in the bus as it takes them to Louisville, Kentucky. This photograph was taken in 1943 by Esther Bubley.

OPPOSITE The cover of this sheet music, which was published circa 1847, shows the character of Jim Crow dancing at the center, with ragged and grinning musicians beside him. These figures are caricatures (exaggerated, unrealistic pictures) of African Americans and reinforced the unfair stereotype that black people were carefree and slow-witted.

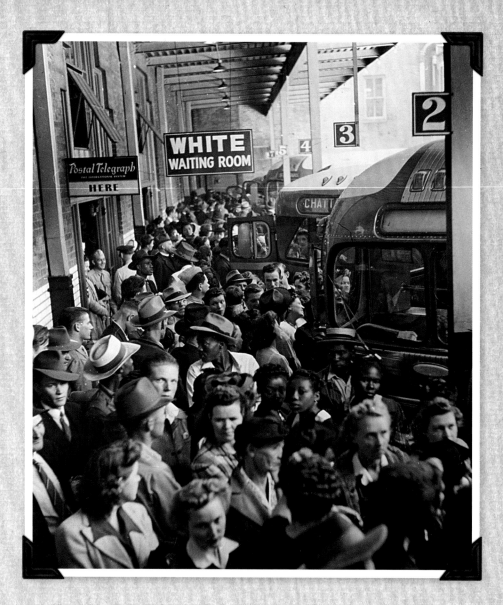

A 1915 South Carolina law said that black and white workers in textile factories could not work in the same room or collect their paychecks from the same window. Mississippi required different taxi services for African Americans and whites. In pet cemeteries in Washington, D.C., dogs owned by white people were buried in a section separate from dogs owned by blacks. In 1914, Louisiana required that blacks and whites enter and leave circuses at different entrances and exits and buy their tickets at separate windows. A 1915 law in Oklahoma called for separate telephone booths for white and black callers.

The entire system of segregation—laws and rules, as well as customs and prejudices about African Americans—came to be called "Jim Crow." Thomas "Daddy" Rice, a white actor, had created a song and dance that he performed while pretending to be a black man—Jim Crow—sometime around 1828. The character Jim Crow was a bundle of stereotypes about African Americans. He wore ragged clothes and shoes with holes in them. He was lazy, comical, and not too bright, and he spoke with an exaggerated accent. The refrain of the song, published in sheet music, read:

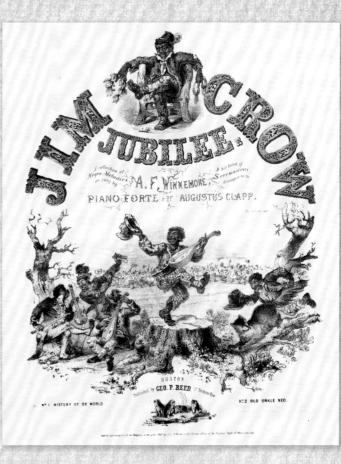

Weel about, and turn about, and do jis so.

Eb'ry time I weel about, I jump Jim Crow.

Jim Crow became a very popular character in minstrel shows—musicals in which white actors pretended to be black by coloring their faces with burnt cork or other substances. By 1838, the term "Jim Crow" was used to refer in general to African Americans. By the 1890s, it described the race-based way of life developing in the South. Jim Crow came to mean "second-class citizen."

African Americans who broke the Jim Crow laws or defied the customs could be put in jail—or be shot at, beaten, or lynched (killed by a mob when they were accused of a crime, without a trial, even if they were innocent). Lynching took the lives of 4,715 black men, women, and children from 1882 to 1946. There were more lynchings in the South than in any other part of the country. These were often public events, sometimes with hundreds of white people looking on, many smiling. White people did not need to hide their crimes; those who killed blacks were rarely arrested. When they were arrested, they frequently were not convicted in court.

Fear and violence were the foundations of the Jim Crow system. Pauli Murray remembered seeing the teenage "John Henry Corniggins lying in the tall grass close to a briar patch" when she was six years old. "He lay on his side," she wrote, "his legs twisted around one another, one hand flung over his head . . . the other crumpled under his body. . . . John Henry lay so still he did not even move to shoo away the large green fly that had settled on his face." The black community suspected John Henry had been shot by a white man for crossing through the man's watermelon patch. No one was ever arrested for the murder.

An African American woman named Joanne told the story of her friend Bobby, who died in 1942 in Georgia. "In many places he went, he passed for white," she said, referring to his light skin. "When [several white men] found out that he [was] a Negro, he was killed. . . . Bobby's body was chained to a car on a gravel road. And they dragged his body until it was unrecognizable. . . . I could see. . . . I happened to be in a car that was on [the] highway . . . that night. . . . It was the Ku Klux Klan because all the people had their heads covered with white sheets. . . . Only thing I know . . . something terrible is happening. . . . We went on about our way, because, you know, okay, you better not stop. Or you are going to get the same thing or worse. . . . When you see something happening and you [are] in the deep South, you [are] afraid to say anything about it, so you are going to hush-hush."

More people were lynched in the South than in any other part of the United States, and the majority of those lynched were black Americans. Here, a huge crowd gathers to watch the lynching of Jesse Washington, an African American teenager, in Waco, Texas, on May 15, 1916.

But some southerners openly opposed lynching. Ida B. Wells, born in Mississippi in 1862, was a black journalist in Memphis, Tennessee, when her friend and two other men, successful grocery store owners, were lynched in 1892. In protest, she advocated that African Americans boycott the Memphis streetcars or leave the area altogether for the West. Soon after, the offices of her newspaper, *Free Speech*, were destroyed, and Wells was forced to move north for her safety. She continued to write and speak out against lynching. Texas-born Jessie Daniel Ames, a white woman, founded the Association of Southern Women for the Prevention of Lynching in 1930, based in Atlanta, Georgia.

Thousands of white members campaigned and lectured in their communities and in places where African Americans had been lynched. With some success, they challenged white sheriffs and judges to pledge that they would do everything they could to protect their prisoners so that these prisoners could receive a fair trial.

To avoid losing their lives, jobs, or homes or being evicted from the land they farmed, however, black people usually accepted Jim Crow. "[We] had to act

Many people, including southerners like Ida B. Wells and Jessie Ames, opposed lynchings. In this photo, a group marches past the Capitol in Washington, D.C., to protest the shooting of four African Americans by a mob in Georgia. Roger and Dorothy Malcom and George and Mae Murray Dorsey, all sharecroppers, were killed at Moore's Ford Bridge in 1946.

. . . just as though everything was all right," said Ned Cobb, whose grandmother had been a slave. "[My family] had to do whatever the white man directed [them] to do, couldn't voice their heart's desire. That was the way of life that I was born and raised into."

In addition to laws, hundreds of unwritten rules kept black and white people so separate in their daily lives that it was hard to know each other beneath the surface—what the other person thought and felt, what they dreamed of achieving. Not only were people segregated, but also the "rules" *always* favored whites over blacks. "We automatically [knew] you went in the back door," explained Cleaster Mitchell, who grew up in Arkansas and worked for a white family. "You didn't have to guess about that. You could work in the house all day. . . . [The] only way you [came] out the front door [was if] you swept the front porch off."

Signs reading "colored" and "white" were posted all over the southern states and the states that bordered them, like Oklahoma. This sign directs African Americans to use a separate water fountain from the one for whites. The photograph was taken in 1939.

African American children learned the way to behave at an early age, although if they had little contact with white people, it might be a while before they realized how strong segregation was. "I didn't understand segregation until I was maybe nine or ten years old, when I was reading and I could see signs saying 'colored' and 'white,'" said Lillian Smith of Wilmington, North Carolina. "You couldn't drink at a [white] water fountain even though you were shopping [with white people] in the same store."

Signs marked "white" or "colored" or "whites only" were everywhere in the South, instant, visible symbols of segregation. Sometimes laws indicated where these signs should be placed. Some laws even said how large or small they should be or the kind and color of paint to be used. But many of the signs went up just because people wanted to emphasize the "unwritten" laws. For African Americans, such signs were a constant reminder that they were second-class citizens. "Colored waiting rooms were everywhere," pointed out David Matthews, who was a child in the 1920s in Indianola, Mississippi. "White and black even in the courthouse. They had a little window where you [went] in and got your tag [license plate] [in a] little dark corner. They would issue tags to the whites way out in the bright lights."

There were no signs to remind blacks and whites how to respond to each other when they met. Custom and habit told them what to say and do. "White men and women were addressed as 'Mr. and Mrs.,'" said Kenneth Young of Alabama. "You didn't address blacks that way." White people often called black men "boy" and black women "auntie" instead of using their proper names. When mail came to the post office in Bolivar County, Mississippi, even as late as the 1930s, the white postal workers would cross out the word "Mr." on an envelope going to a black man. In 1939, African American Eloise Blake was arrested and fined fifteen dollars in Columbia, South Carolina, for asking to speak to "Mrs. Pauline Clay" on the telephone. Mrs. Clay was a maid. Her white employer answered the phone and turned Blake in to the police for using "Mrs." as a courtesy before the name of a black woman.

Jim Crow turned politeness and manners upside down. "During my first year as a Boy Scout, age twelve, I was in downtown Tulsa and spied an elderly white woman . . . attempting to cross the street," wrote the historian John Hope Franklin about his childhood in segregated Oklahoma in the 1920s. "It was obvious that her sight was impaired, and I rushed to help her, thus fulfilling the Boy Scout requirement to do one good deed each day. She eagerly accepted my assistance. However, when we were in the middle of the intersection . . . she asked me if I was white or Negro. When I replied that I was a Negro, she shook my arm loose, commanding me to take my filthy hands off her."

The family of Pomp Hall, a black tenant farmer, is shown eating breakfast together at their home in Creek County, Oklahoma, in 1940. Parents like Mr. Hall, grandparents, black teachers, ministers, and other adults passed on to African American children a sense of self-respect. This photograph was taken by Russell Lee.

How do you fight a system like segregation, which affects every part of your life and makes you feel bad about who you are no matter how well you act? Even in the South, where segregation was the most rigid, African Americans found ways to believe in themselves and to pass on to their children a sense of worth and self-respect. Benjamin Mays, a teacher and clergyman who became the president of Morehouse College, was born in 1894. When he was growing up in Greenwood, South Carolina, his mother told him, "You are as good as anybody!"

She encouraged him to get an education. Charles Evers, raised in Mississippi in the 1920s, learned from his mother that "white people weren't any better than we are, but they sure thought they were." Segregation could not prevent humor and anger, or individual acts of defiance and dignity.

Olivia Cherry, who grew up in Chesapeake, Virginia, showed her independent spirit at the risk of losing her job. The white woman whom she worked for, Cherry said, "would call me. I would be upstairs cleaning the bathroom and she said, 'Susie.' They loved to call me Susie. So I didn't answer. I was a spunky kid then. I was like 13 or 14, and I didn't answer. Finally, she [came] to the steps and said, 'Olivia, you hear me calling you?' I said, 'Now I hear you. Now you said, "Olivia." That's my name.'"

Pauli Murray, who grew up in North Carolina, said, "I carried on my own private protest. I walked almost everywhere to stay off the Jim Crow streetcars and I would not go downtown to the theaters because that meant climbing the back stairs to the colored 'peanut gallery.'" Many African American parents kept their children away from segregated facilities whenever they could and refused to attend segregated performances or sports events.

School, however, was one place that was always segregated. Even young children learned that separate was not equal when they went to school. Everything from buildings to textbooks to teachers' pay was inferior in schools for African Americans compared with those for white people. In 1910 in Beaufort County, the state of South Carolina spent $40.68 to provide education for each white child but only $5.95 for each black child. The average value of a school building for whites was $30,056, but for blacks it was $3,953. That same year in Macon County, the state of Alabama spent $57,385 to educate 1,435 white students and only $27,813 for 7,145 black children.

The elementary school for African American children in South Boston, Virginia, photographed sometime between 1920 and 1940, s a simple wooden building with few windows.

n contrast, the elementary school for white children in South Boston, Virginia—also photographed between 1920 and 1940—is

"I was six [when] I started in the first grade," William J. Croker said. "The first school [I attended] was Waterford Elementary School in south Norfolk, Virginia. This was an eight-room building without a library. We had books without backs on them, pages torn out of them, and some of the pages were marked. . . . What we got was the books from the white schools, which they had probably used for four or five years and then passed on to us." Although some laws said that white and black students could not use the same books, it was common for black schools to receive used texts from white schools—but never the other way around.

Many African American children did not go to school for the full academic year because they were required to work, often for a white employer. "I went to Chehaw elementary [school]," said Ann Pointer, who grew up in the 1930s in Macon County, Georgia. "It was [a] two-room school. One teacher taught [grades] one through three, the other taught four through six. And we could not go to school until October. . . . And you know why? Because Mr. Childer's cotton had to be picked and gathered before the black children went to school. . . . The first two weeks of school we had to clean . . . and get the school in shape. So we really didn't start classes up until November . . . and the first of May school closed. . . .

Many African American children worked much of the year, often at times when they should have been in school. The black children and adults in this postcard pose in a field around the white cotton planter for whom they work. The photo was taken circa 1908 by H. Tees in West Point, Mississippi.

If you [had] a child and the [white] man want[ed] him to work . . . he'd get him out of school and make him go to the field."

Yet even with these inequalities, many men and women who went to segregated schools gave credit to black parents and teachers for trying to give them a decent education. "At I. C. Norcom High School [in Portsmouth, Virginia] there was no gym," remembered John W. Brown, who was born in 1917. "The football team was equipped with the . . . leftover football equipment from the white high school. . . . The only thing that was equal was the caliber of teachers that we had. We had dedicated teachers that went beyond the unequal requirements, because the white schools had [a] curriculum quite different from the black schools. . . . [Trigonometry] was taught in the white schools. It wasn't taught at Norcom. But we had some black teachers that slipped it in."

Black children also learned about their heritage from their elders. Mamie Garvin Fields of Charleston, South Carolina, remembered the difference between when she went to the public school and when she attended "classes" in the informal neighborhood "school" her uncle built in his backyard. There, her cousin Lala taught kids "things that you didn't get at public schools," she said. "I learned about slavery as our relatives had experienced it and what it meant. She taught us how strong our ancestors back in slavery were and what fine people they were. I guess today people would say that was teaching us 'black history.'"

"My grandfather bought Black history books," said Sarah Lee Anderson, who grew up in Palding County, Georgia, in the 1920s and 1930s. "You know . . . back in the 1800's . . . there were Black people that were in Congress . . . that had positions in the Government and that were leaders. And he encouraged us that we could be that; we could do that even though we were not doing it then."

Black children also learned outside the classroom, from their parents and other relatives and adults in their communities. Here, a sharecropping mother teaches her children numbers and letters in their home in Transylvania, Louisiana, in 1939. African American children also learned about black history from their elders, a subject not taught in many schools. This photo was taken by Russell Lee.

Educational psychologist and professor Asa Hilliard, who spent part of his childhood in Texas, appreciated being part of "a strong community. . . . The fact that we were politically segregated, . . . that we simply didn't have the choice to go anywhere other than to [segregated] schools . . . that was a bad system. But it didn't crush us. . . . I went to school—I went to church on Sunday. Most of my teachers were in one of the two or three churches that we would attend. . . . Most of the community activities, everybody was there. . . . The physician lived two blocks away from me and people were poor and rich and they were all in the same community. It's the strong community . . . that accounts for our strengths."

Segregated schools did not stop some African Americans from going to college, to integrated colleges in the North or to historically black colleges like Howard University, in Washington, D.C.; Fisk University, in Nashville, Tennessee; or Tuskegee University, in Alabama. Tuskegee was established in 1880 by the Alabama legislature; Booker T. Washington became its first president in 1881. Washington championed education for black men and women that would qualify them for jobs and help them to advance economically. He was the leading spokesman for African Americans in the 1890s and known throughout the United States. But in the early 1900s, he was increasingly challenged by other black leaders because he did not actively protest against Jim Crow and he compromised with white people who supported segregation.

Nonetheless, Tuskegee graduated black teachers, skilled workers, and businesspeople, as well as farmers, who made a living in the Jim Crow South, where most African Americans had limited choices for work as well as education. Only some white-owned businesses would hire black people. A few African Americans found jobs in the iron and steel industry near Birmingham, Alabama. But as Leon Alexander, who worked in the Alabama coal fields, remembered, "[T]here were things back then . . . called 'a white man's job' and 'a black man's job.' Ninety percent of the machinery was operated by white[s]. The cutting machines [were] one of the few things that [were] predominantly black . . . because that was *really* some tough work. . . . But if it was a machine where you [were] sitting down . . . nine out of ten times . . . it was a white man sitting on that machine."

When John W. Brown applied for a job at the Norfolk Naval Shipyard in Virginia, he had the fifth-highest score out of five thousand people on an apprenticeship exam. "I had applied to be an electrician," he said. "When I got over there, I found out that the electrical shop, mechanics' apprentices and mechanics were all white. They didn't have any black electricians and they didn't intend to have any. So they offered me [a job as an] apprentice plumber, hoping that I would refuse. I accepted it. . . . It was made very clear to me that I was not wanted, which made me more determined to stay. I stayed there for over forty years." By being persistent and not giving up, African Americans like Brown were able to combat Jim Crow.

ABOVE Sometime around 1900, these students were photographed working in the pharmaceutical (medicines and drugs) laboratory at Howard University, a traditionally black college in Washington, D.C. It was founded in 1867 by General Oliver Howard, a Union officer in the Civil War and the head of the Freedmen's Bureau.

LEFT Male and female students study in the library at Fisk University circa 1900. A traditionally black college founded in 1866 in Memphis, Tennessee, the school was named for General Clinton B. Fisk, who worked for the Tennessee Freedmen's Bureau after the Civil War and donated Union army buildings to the new school.

Some African Americans found work in the lumber and timber industries, but they received low wages. Textile mills did not employ blacks but hired white women and children (who also got low wages). Black women were often domestic workers, caring for children and cleaning and cooking meals for white families. Farming was the way most southern blacks made a living, but they usually did not own their farmland outright. They were sharecroppers; they rented land to farm; or they earned wages as a farmhand. The landowners were most often white.

Sharecroppers, tenant farmers, and even wage earners had to borrow from their employers until the crops came in. Thus, they became debtors to those who owned the land and to merchants who sold them basic goods. If a crop was poor—or, in the case of a commercial crop like cotton, if the market price was low—they would not earn enough to pay off the debt. Even if the crop did make money, it was not uncommon for landowners to cheat the sharecropper or tenant of any profit, especially those who had never learned math. "I seen that education was a great thing and something that I badly needed, especially in keeping my accounts," said Timothy Smith, who insisted he have time off at night to go to school before he would sign up to work for a landowner.

Sharecroppers and tenants often lived at the same income level from year to year, never saving enough to improve their lives; or worse, they went deeper into debt. "The way I see it . . . if you don't make enough [money] to have some left you aint done nothin, except given the other fellow your labor," said Ned Cobb, an Alabama sharecropper who farmed in the first part of the twentieth century. "That crop out there goin to prosper enough for him to get his and get what I owe him; he's making his profit but he aint going to let me rise."

Sharecroppers and tenant farmers lived on a piece of the landowner's property. Their homes were usually humble. "My parents were farmers. We had three rooms. There were nine of us," said Walter M. Cavers, who was born in 1910 and grew up in Autauga County, Alabama. "Our house was partly built

OPPOSITE Most southern black people worked in agriculture. These men and women from Memphis, Tennessee, are on a truck that will take them to a plantation in Arkansas, where they will hoe cotton. They will be paid one dollar a day. This photograph was taken in 1937 by Dorothea Lange.

LEFT Many African American southerners were sharecroppers who worked for white owners. They often made only enough money to live on from year to year and were unable to save to buy their own land. This sharecropper and his family lived on the Pettway Plantation in Gee's Bend, Alabama, in 1939.

with slabs. . . . That's the outside of a log." Sometimes, black farmers would be able to grow some vegetables near their houses for their own use; sometimes not, if the landowner wanted only cash crops like cotton and tobacco planted.

For those who lived in towns and cities in the South, housing was almost always segregated. "We have a railroad in Wilson [North Carolina]," George Butterfield Jr. said of the town where he grew up. "The railroad has always been the line of demarcation between black Wilson and white Wilson. . . . When you cross that railroad [from the black side to the white], you could tell you were in another world."

African Americans generally lived in the part of town where houses were smaller, older, and less well maintained. Houses in "the Bottoms," a black section of Knoxville, Tennessee, were "hardly more than rickety shacks clustered on stilts like Daddy Long Legs, along the slimy bank of putrid and evil-smelling 'Cripple Creek,'" recalled James Robinson. In black neighborhoods, the streets were rarely paved. Often, there was no running water, sewer service, or proper drainage; waste collected in yards and streets. African Americans were far more likely than white people to be exposed to and to catch diseases such as tuberculosis and typhoid fever in this environment. Hospitals and health care were segregated. As a group, blacks had less access to medical care. In 1900, the death rate for blacks was 69 percent higher than it was for whites in the city of Atlanta.

Faced with these conditions, African Americans looked to themselves, their neighbors, and their friends for support. Black men's and women's mutual societies were part social clubs, part platforms for calling for political change, and part self-help groups, caring for the sick and the unemployed and paying for hospitalization and burial when needed. "If you [were] a farmer and your mule died and you belonged to the Emancipated Order," A. I. Dixie said of his

No matter how much money they had, black people in cities and towns usually lived in segregated neighborhoods. C. C. Dodson and his family stand outside their home in Knoxville, Tennessee, circa 1899. Mr. Dodson was a jeweler with a good business in Knoxville. He was one of many African Americans who prospered, not only in the late 1800s but also during the 1900s, despite fraternal lodge, "everybody that had a mule had to give you a day's work, until they could get you another mule."

One of the earliest and most successful women's organizations, the National Association of Colored Women (NACW), was founded in 1896. Its motto was "Lifting as We Climb." The largely middle-class members worked to improve the lives of the poor with projects for better education and health, urged black Americans to be thrifty and save money, lobbied against lynching, and advocated civil rights. The NACW was very active in the North, but it also had members in the South.

ABOVE African American members of men's and women's clubs and mutual aid societies provided support to one another during hard times and offered educational and social activities in good ones. These five women are officers of the Women's League of Newport, Rhode Island, circa 1899. Women's organizations like this one also operated in the South.

RIGHT Along with providing religious services, churches were also places where African Americans found support and strength and built communities. This photo of members of the First Congregational Church in Atlanta, Georgia, was taken in 1899 or 1900 by Thomas E. Askew, a prominent black photographer in Atlanta.

African Americans could also turn to their churches for help and uplift. Black Americans had formed their own churches, separate from whites, as early as 1793, when the African Methodist Episcopal (AME) Church began in Philadelphia. What black people couldn't find in the towns and plantations of the South, they found in church: the chance to be leaders and organizers and to take pride in their own institutions. Churches provided a safe haven where they could give and receive social and economic support, discuss politics, fund education, and be at ease without having to worry about segregation for a while.

Church was the center of Dovey Roundtree's childhood. She was born in Charlotte, North Carolina, in 1914. "My father died early, when I was four, and we went to live with Grandma Rachel and Grandpa Graham. He was pastor of East Stonewall Church. . . . [The church] was filled with activity. . . . I made my first speech when I was three. I don't know what I said, but that's what Mama told me, and people cheered." Even when her grandfather was transferred to another church, she said, she and her mother "continued there because it was near our home, and that's where I got all . . . the little things that you need . . . to go forward, to look upward."

Baptisms were a spiritual and a social event. Those baptized were often adults, and in most southern churches they waded into lakes or rivers to be immersed in water for the ceremony. This baptism took place in South Carolina sometime between 1900 and 1906.

Ministers encouraged churchgoers to keep up their spirits; they often spoke to white leaders on behalf of the black community. Services and baptisms drew communities together. Maggie Dulin, who grew up in Muhlenburg County, Kentucky, remembered "one of the most beautiful baptizings you ever saw. . . . The water just glittered." Those to be baptized entered the water wearing white robes and scarves. "And the man that baptized us, he was a really noted singer, and he started singing 'Wade in the Water.' Oh! . . . That was the prettiest thing I ever heard in my life."

African American ministers, as well as teachers, doctors, lawyers, land and business owners, and other professionals, challenged the idea that black people were poor, unsuccessful, and uneducated. But middle-class and wealthier

African Americans also lived under segregation and also risked violence. When Henry Watson, a well-to-do Georgia farmer, drove into town in a new car in the early twentieth century, whites poured gasoline on the car and set it on fire. In 1917, a newspaper in Macon, Georgia, wrote about four different African American car owners who had been beaten by white people and told to get rid of their automobiles.

African Americans might be able to afford eating in restaurants or staying in hotels, but they were not allowed in most of these establishments. By refusing to admit any black person, white people were reminding *all* African Americans of how inferior they were. George Butterfield Jr.'s father was a dentist with a successful practice, and the first black admitted to the all-white North Carolina Dental Society. He liked to travel with his family to conventions and meetings. "In the old, old days, we would have to stay in rooming houses," Butterfield remembered. "We would go into a town. We would find a black community, and we would find the local boarding house and that's where we would stay. Hotels were unheard of for black people. That was basically in the South and in the Midwest. . . . If we went to Atlanta, Birmingham, Nashville, we would have to find a boarding house. When we needed to eat, we couldn't just pull up to a restaurant. . . . We would have [to] come off the highway and drive into town . . . and find the local black café."

Even famous black people could not stay in hotels or eat in restaurants. Irene Monroe owned a nightclub in Bessemer, Alabama, in the 1940s. The blues guitarist and singer B. B. King and the singer and composer Ray Charles were among those who came to perform. "That's when I got [a] little old building out there as a motel," Monroe said. "I had to fix a place for them to stay, because they couldn't stay in the white motel."

'The Green Book helps solve your travel problems'

By Wendell P. Alston, Special Representative, Esso Standard Oil Co.

Through the ages, men of all races have moved from place to place. Some to seek new lands, others to avoid persecution or intolerance and still others for the sake of adventure.

Today, men of all races continue to move and for much the same reasons, though since the days of the foot-traveler and the ox-cart, they travel with much more convenience and comfort and at far greater speed.

For most travelers, whether they travel in modern high-speed motor cars, streamlined Diesel-powered trains, luxurious ocean liners or globe encircling planes, there are hotels of all sizes and classes, waiting and competing for their patronage. Pleasure resorts in the mountains and at the sea shore beckon him. Roadside inns and cabins spot the highways and all are available if he has the price.

For some travelers however, the facilities of many of these places are not available, even though they may have the price, and any traveler to whom they are not available, is thereby faced with many and sometimes difficult problems.

The Negro traveler's inconveniences are many and they are increasing because today so many more are traveling, individually and in groups.

This year for the annual convention of the largest Negro organization in the world, nine special trains in addition to the regularly scheduled trains of a number of railroads were required to transport more than fifty thousand of its members to a mid-western city. Several more thousands made the trip by car and some by plane.

Top ranking orchestras and numerous minor ones, concert singers and various musical organizations are moving over the country in increasing numbers. Touring clubs, like the one in the nation's capital which chartered three of the most modern buses of one of the country's largest bus lines for a trip to California and Mexico this year, are growing in number. More students and teachers and many others in the field of education seeking further training in the country's major centers of learning are traveling. More business men, representing increasing Negro enterprises, are traveling from city to city, and more white corporations cognizant of the mounting purchasing power of the Negro consumer, have Negro representatives in the field, a number of whom, like ourselves, spend half the year traveling.

ABOVE This is the introductory page from *The Negro Motorist Green Book* of 1949. Victor H. Green, a postal worker in Harlem, New York, who was also active in political affairs, started the *Green Book* in 1936 to let African Americans know where they would be welcomed when they traveled to different cities across the United States. Many hotels and restaurants would not allow black people to use their facilities.

BELOW This page from *The Negro Motorist Green Book* of 1949 shows places open to black travelers in cities and towns of Connecticut and Delaware. *The Green Book* listed both hotels and "tourist homes," private houses that would take in guests. It also included beauty salons and barbershops, gas stations, and nightclubs where people could go for entertainment.

BRIDGEPORT

HOTELS
Y. W. C. A.—Golden Hill St.
TOURIST HOMES
Mrs. M. Barrett—85 Summer St.
Mrs. E. Lawrence—68 Fulton St.
GARAGES
W & T—179 William St.

HARTFORD

HOTELS
Parrish Rooming House—26 Walnut St.
TOURIST HOMES
Mrs. Johnson—2016 Main St.
BEAUTY SHOPS
Quaility—1762 Main St.
BARBER SHOPS
Williams—1978 Main Street
TAVERNS
Turf Club—2243 Main St.
NIGHT CLUBS
TURF CLUB INCORPORATED OF CONN.—2243 MAIN STREET

NEW HAVEN

HOTELS
Phillis Wheatley—108 Canal Street
TOURIST HOMES
Dr. M. F. Allen—65 Dixwell Avenue
Mrs. C. Raone—68 Dixwell Avenue
RESTAURANTS
Monterey—267 Dixwell Ave.
Belmonts—156 Dixwell Ave.

ZING THESE PLACES

BEAUTY PARLORS
Mme. Ruby—175 Goffe St.
Harris—138 Goffe St.
Glady's—624 Orchard Street
Ethel's—152 Dixwell Avenue
Harris—734 Orchard St.
SCHOOL OF BEAUTY CULTURE
Modern—170 Goffe St.
NIGHT CLUBS
Elk's—204 Goffe St.
Lillian's Paradise—137 Wallace St.

NEW LONDON

TOURIST HOMES
Hempstead Cottage— 73 Hempstead St.
Mrs. E. Whittle—785 Bank St.

STAMFORD

HOTELS
GLADSTONE—Gay St.
TOURIST HOMES
Robert Graham—37 Hanrahan Ave.
NIGHT CLUBS
Sizone—136 W. Main St.

WATERBURY

TOURIST HOMES
Mrs. A. Dunham—208 Bridge St.
Community House—34 Hopkins St.

WEST HAVEN

HOTELS
Seaview—392 Beach St.
TAVERNS
Hoot Owl—374 Beach St.

DELAWARE

DOVER

HOTELS
Dean's—Forrest St.
Mosely's—Division St.
Weston's—Division St.

LAUREL

RESTAURANTS
Joe Randolph's—W. 6th St.
BARBER SHOPS
Joe Randolph's—W. 6th St.
BEAUTY PARLORS
Orchid—W. 6th St.

TOWNSEND

HOTELS
Rodney—Dupont Highway-Rt. 13
GARAGES
Hood's—Dupont Hiway

The Hotel Clark was one of the segregated hotels in Memphis, Tennessee, that would accept African American guests. Its sign advertises "the best service for colored only." Marion Post Wolcott took the photograph in 1939.

The racial riots in Tulsa, Oklahoma, in 1921 destroyed African American houses and businesses. Much of the violence was aimed at middle-class and professional black people. This photograph, taken by the Alvin C. Krupnick Company, shows the smoking ruins of homes destroyed by fire.

Prosperity did not stop African Americans from becoming the victims of racial riots. For some three or four days in 1906 in Atlanta, Georgia, white mobs rioted, fueled by unfounded rumors of black violence against white women. The rioters killed at least ten African Americans; some historians estimate that twenty-five to forty black people died. Two white people also died. The mobs beat and injured dozens more African Americans and burned black homes and black-owned businesses. They especially targeted middle-class neighborhoods.

Fifteen years later, in 1921, white mobs rioted against the black community of Tulsa, Oklahoma. "The building where I had my office was a smoldering ruin," remembered Buck Colbert Franklin, an African American lawyer. "All my lawbooks and office fixtures had been consumed by flames. I went to where my roominghouse had stood . . . but it was in ashes, with all my clothes and the money to be used in moving my family. As far as one could see, not a Negro dwellinghouse or place of business stood."

This was Jim Crow's message in the South: African Americans were not to prosper. After the Atlanta riot, W. E. B. Du Bois, an African American sociologist and a professor at Atlanta University, wrote: "If my own city . . . [was] offered . . . the choice between 500 Negro college graduates—forceful, busy, ambitious men of property and self-respect—and 500 black . . . vagrants and criminals, the popular vote in favor of the criminals would be simply overwhelming. Why? because they want Negro crime? No, not that they fear Negro crime less, but that they fear Negro ambition and success more. . . . The South can conceive neither machinery nor place for the educated, self-reliant, self-assertive black man."

Du Bois did not accept this situation. He was one of the black activists who, together with white activists who opposed segregation, established the National Association for the Advancement of Colored People (NAACP) in 1909. It was the leading civil rights organization of the first half of the twentieth century. The NAACP sued against segregated schools and accommodations and held marches and protests. It was headquartered in New York City, and most of its members lived in the North. But James Weldon Johnson—who later became the first black man to head the NAACP—organized nearly fifty local branches in the South between 1916 and 1919. Atlanta, home to several black universities and colleges, had one of the strongest. In the 1920s and 1930s, integrated Southern groups opposing racism included the Commission on Interracial Cooperation (which became the Southern Regional Council) and the Southern Conference for Human Welfare.

If an African American wanted to stay in the South but avoid the daily trials of segregation, he or she could live in one of the all-black towns that grew up during and after Reconstruction. Eatonville, Florida, founded in 1887, was the first incorporated black community in the United States. Edwin McCabe started Langston, Oklahoma, in 1890. Isaiah Montgomery founded Mound Bayou in the Mississippi Delta in 1887. "Everything here was Negro, from the symbols of law and authority and the man who ran the bank down to the fellow who drove the road scraper," remembered a black resident who had lived in Mound Bayou as a boy. "That gave us kids a sense of security and power and pride that colored kids didn't get anywhere else." These towns and dozens like them offered alternatives to the narrow life most whites allowed blacks in the South. But African Americans also traveled north and west in the hope of finding greater opportunity and freedom.

OPPOSITE The NAACP organized protests and demonstrations to speak out against segregation and for equal opportunities. In 1947, these young members of the NAACP march with signs protesting segregation laws in Houston, Texas. Years before the better-known civil rights movement of the late 1950s and 1960s, African Americans were demanding justice and civil rights.

ABOVE This young black girl plays a singing game in Eatonville, Florida, one of the all-black towns founded in the South. Children in towns like Eatonville did not have to face legal segregation every day. This photograph was taken by Alan Lomax in 1935.

After the Civil War, many African Americans moved away from the South in search of better opportunities. The number migrating to northern cities grew after 1900. These boys were photographed in the South Side of Chicago in 1941 by Russell Lee. Chicago's black population jumped from about 44,000 people in 1910 to about 234,000 people in 1930.

THE
NORTH

Jim Crow didn't make its home only in the South.
It was active in the North—those states in the northern, midwestern, and western parts of the United States, from Maine to New York, from Ohio to California. Although the segregation rules in the North weren't always as clear as they were in the South, discrimination and prejudice found a place in every part of the country from the 1890s to the 1950s.

"There were no signs 'colored' and 'white,'" said Anna Arnold Hedgeman, a civil rights activist who grew up in Minnesota. "But the wall of separation was as vivid in the minds of Negroes and whites as though the signs were present." In 1924, Hedgeman took a job at the Young Women's Christian Association in Springfield, Ohio. Springfield was not a southern city. In fact, it had been a center for the movement to abolish slavery before the Civil War. After the war, many white people in Springfield supported the Republican Party, which ended slavery and granted civil rights to the freedmen.

Many African Americans moved from the South to Springfield for better jobs and greater freedom. When Hedgeman arrived, almost eight thousand black people lived there. But between 1900 and 1921, three anti-black race riots had upset the city, and by 1924, some three thousand whites were members of a Springfield-based chapter of the Ku Klux Klan. Restaurants and theaters

were segregated by custom, and black children attended a different school from white children, even though school segregation was illegal in Ohio.

Why did African Americans leave the South for places like Springfield, Ohio? "I [have] been here all my life but would be glad to go where I can educate my children where they can be of service to themselves, and this will never be here," said a black worker in Alexandria, Louisiana, who thought of moving to Chicago. An African American from Greenville, Mississippi, wanted "to get [his] family out of this cursed south land down here a negro man is not as good as a white man's dog." A teacher from Lexington, Mississippi, was "compelled to teach 150 children without any assistance" while getting paid only about one-quarter of what a white teacher made working with thirty children.

"After twenty years of seeing my people lynched for any offense from spitting on the sidewalk to stealing a mule, I made up my mind that I would turn the prow of my ship toward the part of the country where the people at least made a pretense at being civilized," said a man who settled in Chicago. A black newspaper in Savannah, Georgia, wrote, "The most universal reason given [for migrating north] has been the terror of physical violence, this even outweighing the security of property and the failure of justice in the courts."

Between 1900 and 1940, some 1.8 million African Americans traveled north and west. They left the South for better jobs, for better education for their children, and to be treated humanely and with respect. They left to escape rigid segregation, lynching, and other racial violence. This was called the Great Migration. Some historians divide it into two parts: the First Great Migration (through World War I) and the Second Great Migration (through World War II and sometimes beyond, through the 1960s). During the United States' involvement in these wars, the need for more industrial workers in factories outside the South drew particularly high numbers of black migrants.

In 1910, approximately 84,000 African Americans lived in Philadelphia, according to the U.S. Census. By 1920, there were more than 134,000 blacks living there, and by 1930, more than 219,000. The number in Cleveland, Ohio, jumped from about

OPPOSITE During the Great Migration, African Americans moved north and west for better jobs and better education and to escape racial violence. This group of migrants from Florida drive a packed car to Cranbury, New Jersey, for work. They were photographed on their way, near Shawboro, North Carolina, in 1940 by Jack Delano.

ABOVE This eleven-year-old newspaper delivery boy, Roland, was among those African Americans growing up in the North. He lived in Newark, New Jersey. Black children had a chance of going to schools with white children in northern cities, but they may have had jobs as well to help their families. Lewis Hine, a well-known photographer of working children, took this photograph in 1924.

African Americans who went north sometimes opened their own businesses, often serving black communities. This grocery and delicatessen in Harlem, New York, was photographed by Aaron Siskind circa 1940.

8,000 in 1910 to about 34,000 in 1920, and about 71,000 in 1930. Buffalo, New York, had some 1,700 black residents in 1910, 4,500 in 1920, and 13,500 in 1930.

Was life better for black Americans in the North? The answer is yes and no. Northern blacks did not have to live with the legal thicket of state and local segregation laws. The constitutions of northern states didn't have provisions that kept black men and women from voting. Some restaurants, theaters, hotels, and libraries were open to them. They had a chance to make a higher salary than they had made in the South. "There is a difference," said Rebecca Stone of her life in Detroit, Michigan, "because in Alabama, at the time, white and coloreds wasn't going to school together. Well, here, at some schools, they do. . . . And here you could eat at the restaurants with the white people. In Alabama you couldn't."

"I was made first assistant to the head carpenter[.] I should have been here [the North] 20 years ago," wrote an African American living in Chicago in 1917 to his family in Hattiesburg, Mississippi. "My children are going to the same school with the whites and I don't have to [be humble] to no one. I have registered, will vote the next election and there isn't any 'yes sir' and 'no sir'— its all yea and no and Sam and Bill."

Yet for African Americans who left the South in search of a better life, the North did not always offer a warm welcome. "You'd be astonished to see just how high race prejudice runs in the North. It is fearful," Clarisa Sledge, who had moved to New York from the South, wrote to Charles N. Hunter in North Carolina in 1904. Asa Hilliard, who as a young person had traveled back and forth between Texas and Colorado, said, "You had basically a segregated society in both places. . . . While on the one hand we were in school with White children, Asian children, [and] Mexican children in the Denver public schools, Denver was still a segregated society. There were places that we couldn't go in hotels; there were amusement parks that we couldn't go to; swimming pools that we couldn't go to; jobs that we couldn't get. The school system itself was not officially segregated but virtually all the Black children went to schools in the Black community."

Some northern and western states had laws segregating schools, but many schools were unofficially segregated because African Americans lived in different neighborhoods from white people. Children therefore often went to local schools that were nearly all-black or all-white. These African American boys play basketball at the Columbus School in Binghamton, New York, in 1937.

Several states in the North, Midwest, and West also had segregation laws on their books. There were laws forbidding white people from marrying African Americans or, sometimes, any person of color. In 1908, the state of Wyoming prohibited "all marriages of white persons with Negroes, Mulattos [people of both black and white descent], Mongolians [Chinese people] or Malaya[ns] [people from the Philippines]." In 1909, Montana passed a law that any white person marrying an African American, Chinese, or Japanese person could be fined five hundred dollars or jailed for one month. After they were fined or jailed, the white person and the person of color could not continue to live together as a legally married couple.

African Americans migrated north and west to escape a Jim Crow education for their children, yet nearly one-quarter of states outside the South had laws segregating black and white students in schools at various times before 1954. In 1902, California, in addition to black children, added Chinese and Japanese students to the groups that could not attend a white school. Kentucky, in 1904, specified that if a school or college wanted to teach both white and black students, they must be in "separate and distinct branch[es], in a different locality, not less than 25 miles apart." A 1905 Kansas law left it up to individual schools to decide whether students would be segregated. A 1933 North Dakota law targeted American Indians, saying that it would not be a good idea "to have Indian children mingle with the white children . . . by reason of the vastly different temperament and . . . other differences and difficulties of the two races." State law in Indiana allowed schools to be segregated until 1949. Several states in the North had antidiscrimination laws, which made segregating schoolchildren illegal, but local school boards still frequently separated black and white students. Often the school boards assigned children to all-black or all-white schools without a choice. This was true in Chester, Pennsylvania, which set up segregated elementary schools in 1912, segregated middle schools in 1929, and segregated high schools in 1934.

In New York state, separate schools for black and white students in rural areas were legal until 1938. Hillburn, about thirty miles from New York City, had a black school, the Brook School, and a white school, the Main School. The Brook School consisted of three rooms in a run-down building that didn't have indoor toilets until 1943. The Main School had a library, a music room, and a gym. In 1943, black parents boycotted the Brook School; they appealed to the New York state commissioner for education for permission to enroll in the white school. The commissioner ordered that the Main School be integrated. Soon after, the white parents refused to send their children to Main, enrolling them in church-run schools instead.

The NAACP fought against school segregation laws in local and state courts—and the Supreme Court. During the 1922–23 school year, for example, black parents boycotted the black school in Springfield, Ohio. The NAACP sued the school district for breaking Ohio's laws. In Philadelphia, New York City, and Chicago, as well as many smaller cities, black parents, with help from the NAACP, protested having their kids attend all-black schools.

Yet integrated schools did not protect black students from discrimination or racial hostility. "I was the only black on the basketball team [in high school]," said Edward Temple, who was born in 1927 and grew up in Harrisburg, Pennsylvania. "We had about three or four [black players] on the football team. We had about four or five on the track team. But we were way, way in the minority. . . . We played football games in Hershey, Pennsylvania, when the cheerleaders got up and, and cheered, 'Get that n_____.' . . . In Shamokin, Pennsylvania, one of the coal mine towns . . . as we got off the bus, they would count, one, two, three . . . and they'd holler 'eight n_____ on the team.' . . .

You'd hear it just go right down the block. 'Eight n_____ on the team.' . . . In the forties, there was a whole [lot of] this in Pennsylvania. . . . You would think, oh, this would happen in Tennessee or Mississippi. . . . But it happens in Pennsylvania too."

African American students in integrated schools often were not supported in following their ambitions and dreams. "I'd just entered high school and I said I wanted to . . . go into radio," remembered Joe Adams, who was born in 1924 and grew up in Los Angeles, California. "My counselor told me that I couldn't go into radio. . . . I wanted to take public speaking. They wouldn't allow me to take public speaking because, years later, I discovered they felt it was for my own good. Take public speaking and then when I get outta school, there was no place to use it. . . . So they told me to take auto shop." But Adams resisted the stereotype of black people as laborers. He pursued his career on his own. "Public speaking was what I wanted, and for that reason I used to go into vacant lots, take the newspaper, read it aloud for elocution and diction, and when given

PEABODY CONSERVATORY OF MUSIC
MT. VERNON PLACE AND CHARLES STREET
BALTIMORE, MD.

CONSERVATORY OFFICE
VIRGINIA CARTY, Secretary

HAROLD RANDOLPH, Director

February 22, 1926.

Cornelius Washington,
1333 Chapel St.,
Norfolk, Va.

Dear Sir:

      I am sorry, but no colored students are accepted at the Peabody Conservatory.

Very truly yours,

Henrietta N. Fuss

OPPOSITE The NAACP fought against school segregation, sometimes by holding protests, often by suing for integrated schools in state courts. The organization welcomed young members. Here, a group of NAACP "Juniors," young drummers and majorettes, pose in front of a church in Santa Clara County, California, sometime between 1930 and 1950.

LEFT This 1926 letter from the Peabody Conservatory of Music in Baltimore, Maryland, tells a student that he can't follow his dream to study music because he is black. Even in places where African American children went to school with white children, white teachers and counselors often discouraged them from pursuing professional careers.

the opportunity I started hanging around the radio stations." He became a well-known disc jockey, actor, and music manager whose clients included Ray Charles.

What was it like for black people who came north not only for education but also for better employment? The vast majority of African Americans who migrated to the North from the South left farming behind and lived in cities. In the years before World War I, men found work as waiters, hotel porters, and janitors. Black women worked in domestic service as maids and laundresses. A *Detroit Free Press* editorial in 1917 observed that the city was "beginning to have a noticeable increase of dark-skinned toilers. These appear to be performing the hard labor of the community, the class of work that calls for muscular effort and no training."

African Americans were denied many jobs, especially those requiring skilled labor—such as mechanic, plumber, electrician, and machine operator—and often found it difficult to move up the economic ladder. Even if he had the skill suited to industry and construction, "the Negro comes up against a problem he has never had to face before, and that is union labor," said the NAACP's James Weldon Johnson in 1918. "In the North, in almost every field the unions shut him out, and he finds himself in the position of an independent or a scab [strikebreaker]. Many colored men skilled in their trades have had to turn to common labor because they were not allowed to join unions." During strikes, black men desperate for work would temporarily take over jobs performed by unionized whites. This created great tension between black and white workers and became part of the negative stereotypes about blacks. Many white workers saw African Americans as competitors for their jobs, whether they were strikebreakers or not; and because of racial prejudice, they did not want to work with black people.

Many African American women who moved to the North or West found jobs as maids, laundresses, or janitors. This woman, posing

African Americans were often treated unfairly at jobs in the North. Here, a group pickets the Mid-City Realty Company in Chicago for better wages. One man carries a sign that reads, "Slavery was abolished—yet we work for $8 a week." This photo was taken by John Vachon in 1941.

In some places, African Americans were paid less for doing the same jobs as white people. Soon after blues performer and composer Bill Broonzy moved to Chicago from Arkansas in 1920, he wrote this song:

> Me an' a white man working side by side,
>
> This is what it meant,
>
> He was getting a dollar an hour,
>
> I was getting fifty cents.
>
> If you white, you all right,
>
> If you brown, stick around,
>
> But if you black, oh buddy,
>
> Get back, get back, get back.

"On receiving jobs in the North, the Negro is given the worst," Bill Smedley wrote in *The Black Worker* of August–September 1936, discussing the situation for African Americans in the automobile industries of Detroit. "There are very few Negroes operating machines. They are either cleaning the floors, machines, etc., or out in the steel yard. Therefore, their wages are considerably lower than the white workers' because they 'can't' operate the machine."

New organizations were formed in response to widespread job discrimination. In 1910, the Committee on Urban Conditions Among Negroes (which, by 1920, had become the National Urban League) was founded to provide support for blacks living in cities, train social workers to work in black communities, and campaign to combat racial prejudice and to expand employment opportunities. Members of the National Negro Congress, founded in 1936, also demonstrated against segregated workplaces and supported decent wages for farmworkers.

Organizations like the National Urban League helped African Americans to find good employment. In the first decades of the Great Migration, labor unions would not allow blacks to join. But by the late 1940s, when this poster was created, the Congress of Industrial Organizations (CIO), a group of many unions, accepted black people and spoke out against discrimination. Milton Ackoff designed the poster.

World War I opened more industrial jobs to blacks, because white labor was in short supply. White men went off to fight, but black men who tried to enlist were not accepted (although they were eventually drafted). When returning white soldiers wanted their jobs back in industries and factories, however, African Americans were the first workers to be let go. Blacks suffered especially during the Great Depression of the 1930s, which was hard on all Americans economically. This was a time when many banks, businesses, and factories closed and people of all colors were out of work. They had no money

Although more African Americans were unemployed during the Great Depression than whites, it was difficult for both white and black people to find a job. Here, out-of-work men receive food on an integrated "soup line" in Chicago in 1930. Soup and bread lines were organized by charities, churches, and the government to feed the many, many people who could not afford to feed themselves.

to buy the goods that factories produced—forcing more factories to close and more people to lose their jobs. By 1932, 25 percent of Americans were unemployed. But there were many more unemployed black people than white people—more than 50 percent of black workers had no job in 1932. In 1931, the National Urban League studied 106 cities. It found that African Americans in those cities had a 30 to 60 percent higher chance of being out of work than white Americans. To help raise black employment, the National Urban League in 1934 organized "Workers Councils" to campaign for opening up labor unions to African Americans.

The American economy began to improve in the late 1930s. African Americans again left the South in large numbers, moving north and west. But they still faced job discrimination. One manager of an aircraft factory in Los Angeles told the Negro National Congress, "I regret to say that it is not the policy of this company to employ people other than that of the Caucasian race." Organizations like the National Urban League picketed and held mass rallies against job discrimination across the country. As in World War I, the shortage of white workers during World World II opened up many jobs for African American men and women. But following the war's end, as white soldiers returned, black men—and women, white and black—once again lost a large number of these jobs.

Through good times and tough times, black churches provided support for northerners, as they did for southerners. For one thing, they helped African Americans find work. "It was not uncommon at a Sunday-morning service for the church clerk to announce that a brother who was an experienced plasterer had just arrived in the city and needed employment; or that a woman, a good cook, would like a job," said Charlotta Bass, who arrived in Los Angeles in 1910 and became the owner and editor of a newspaper, the *California Eagle*. "Church was not only a place of worship; it was likewise the social, civic, and political headquarters where the people assembled for spiritual guidance, *and* civic analyses, political discussions, and social welfare talks and lectures."

African American churches lent money to black people who wanted to start a business but could not get loans from a white bank. They sponsored many youth programs, often training the leaders of the future. During the Great Depression and the 1940s, the People's Independent Church of Christ in Los Angeles provided relief for the unemployed. "I consider it a sin to stand up in the pulpit and preach to hungry people and not help them to get a job or get some food," said the pastor, Reverend Clayton Russell.

RIGHT Children kneel at a Catholic mass in this photograph taken by Jack Delano in 1942 in Chicago. They attend a church segregated by custom (not by law). Like those in the South, northern churches were community centers that provided financial and social help, as well as spiritual guidance, to their members.

OPPOSITE African Americans suffered from housing discrimination. Real estate agents, home owners, and landlords kept them away from "white neighborhoods." In this 1950s photograph, a white crowd gathers outside a home where black people are trying to move in.

Black churches helped to build communities when migrants to northern and western cities found themselves living in "black" neighborhoods. In the early part of the twentieth century, African Americans had more freedom in where they settled and often lived in the same areas as white people. Many of the early migrants to Los Angeles, for example, were middle-class people, who "had come . . . with ready cash," said one resident of the city. In 1910, 36 percent of black families in Los Angeles were home owners. But as the number of African Americans in a community increased, the places where they could live grew more restricted. In 1912, Mr. and Mrs. C. A. Bywater, a black couple, moved into a wealthy white area in California. "Twelve prominent citizens" came to see them, according to the *Crisis*, the NAACP magazine. One of these white people declared, "'I come from Texas . . . where the N_____s have no rights. You've got to get out.'"

A neighborhood might become, or remain, "white" or "black" for many reasons. "Restrictive covenants," which said that certain neighborhoods were

restricted to white people, were widely used from the 1920s through the end of World War II. The white people in a neighborhood would decide that black people could not buy homes there. Rules about this were then written into deeds declaring who could be sold a particular house and who could live in it. Most of these rules kept African Americans from buying a home in an area where many white people lived.

In 1927, the Capitol Hill development in Seattle, Washington, issued a covenant in which people who were selling houses agreed "that no part of the lands owned by them shall ever be used or occupied by, or sold, conveyed, leased, rented or given to Negroes or any person of Negro blood." The same year, the Chicago Real Estate Board adopted a covenant to keep African Americans from buying in "white" neighborhoods. Even when a white community had no

In 1942 the city of Detroit, with funding from the federal government, planned to open a housing project, called Sojourner Trut Homes, for black as well as white people. Whites protested. They erected this sign, topped by two American flags, with their demand that only "white tenants" live in the community. The photo was taken by Arthur Siegel.

A riot erupted at the Sojourner Truth Homes in 1942 as black families tried to move into some of the houses and whites demonstrated against them. Although white people were rioting, almost everyone arrested was African American— including this man, who is being carried by police on a street near the project. The photo is by Arthur Siegel.

restrictive covenants, white real estate agents would not show houses owned by whites to black buyers. Blacks were steered away to neighborhoods where other black people lived, and those neighborhoods tended to be the poorest, most crowded, and most run-down in a city.

During the 1930s and 1940s, the federal government built housing for people with low incomes, but most of these public housing programs were segregated. In 1942, the city of Detroit planned to open a new project, the Sojourner Truth Homes, to African Americans as well as white people. White people objected, and housing officials gave in to their demands. But black people protested the officials' decision and picketed the site of the project. White people began picketing too, and put up a billboard that announced, "WE WANT WHITE TENANTS IN OUR WHITE COMMUNITY." On February 28, some black families moved into the Sojourner Truth Homes. A crowd of black and white demonstrators—the blacks for integration, the whites against it— had to be dispersed by police. They arrested 220 people, almost all of them black. Ironically, the community was named for Sojourner Truth, an African American woman who was a noted abolitionist and women's rights activist.

Many black families could afford to live in areas that were not segregated, but middle-class African Americans suffered from housing discrimination as much as poor blacks did. When the famous baseball player Jackie Robinson and his wife, Rachel, looked for a house to buy in Connecticut in 1953, they were taken "through large derelict buildings . . . and too small cottages," Mrs. Robinson said. "I began to question the [real estate] brokers about their preselection process. One readily admitted that she had picked areas where in her judgment my children would feel 'comfortable.' I wondered how she knew where my children would be comfortable. I suspected she meant not in her backyard."

"There isn't any good private housing for Negroes," said Madison Jones, who lived in New York City in 1951. After he and his wife "saw one advertisement for an uptown apartment at $55 [per month]," he said, "the girl at the real estate office didn't look up when I asked if the apartment was still available. She just said 'Yes' and then she saw us. 'Oh—it's not for colored,' she said."

Madison Jones worked at the headquarters of the NAACP. The organization assisted African Americans who protested against segregated housing and brought some of their cases to court. In 1948, the Supreme Court decided, in *Shelley v. Kraemer*, that restrictive covenants based on race could not be used to keep blacks out of "white" neighborhoods. Roscoe Johnson and his wife moved into their home in a white neighborhood of Chicago in July of the following year. "We didn't put the lights on in the house," Mrs. Johnson said. "We stayed downstairs in the room next to the kitchen. We barricaded the doors with the furniture and put a mattress behind it. We crawled on our hands and knees when the missiles started coming in through the windows. Then they started to throw gasoline-soaked rags stuck in pop bottles. . . . The police did not try to push the crowd away from the house until we heard a riot car screaming."

Housing discrimination in the North could lead to threats and violence. But the gathering together of African Americans in northern and western cities could also produce creative and proud communities. Some black people, in fact, were attracted to the idea of a separate black nation—within the United States or in Africa—made up of strong, independent, all-black businesses, organizations, schools, and training centers. They believed that America would never be an integrated country where all people had equal rights and equal opportunities.

One of these people was Marcus Garvey, who was born on the island of Jamaica and moved to the United States in 1916. He had established the Universal Negro Improvement and Conservation Association and African Communities League (now known as the UNIA) in his own country; in 1917, he formed a branch of the UNIA in Harlem, New York. "A race without authority and power is a race without respect," Garvey declared. What counted was "not justice, but strength." People of African descent should be proud of their race and heritage.

Garvey's ideas appealed to tens of thousands of African Americans who read his newspaper, *Negro World*, and joined branches of the UNIA established across the country—including the South—and in the Caribbean. Members met weekly in "Liberty Halls." Elma Lewis, who grew up in Boston, recalled that "every Sunday the children of that community went to the Universal Negro Improvement Association to improve. We didn't go to the beach. . . . And I can remember all the speeches. The very first thing I remember . . . was a speech . . . about the beauty of Black women." Members in various divisions of the UNIA, such as the Black Cross Nurses and the African Legion, wore uniforms and marched in frequent parades. UNIA's message of black pride and progress was enormously popular in the early 1920s.

Also in the 1920s, the coming together of black artists, writers, and musicians in Harlem flowered into what became known as the Harlem Renaissance. In 1925, educator and philosopher Alain Locke, who headed the philosophy department at Howard University, published *The New Negro: An Interpretation of Negro Life.* This book contained articles by sociologists W. E. B. Du Bois and Charles S. Johnson, and poems by Countee Cullen, Langston Hughes, and Arna Bontemps. Other prominent Harlem Renaissance figures included novelist and folklorist Zora Neale Hurston and novelists Jessie Fauset and Jean Toomer; sculptor Augusta Savage, illustrator Aaron Douglas, and painter William H. Johnson; and bandleader Duke Ellington and pianist Fats Waller, who were both composers of jazz pieces who became internationally famous. White people came in large numbers to hear jazz performed at Harlem's Savoy Ballroom, Apollo Theater, and Cotton Club. (At the Cotton Club black people could perform but not sit in the audience.)

Norma Miller, born in 1919, found growing up in Harlem to be "wonderful.

. . . Everybody came to Harlem. Harlem was the Renaissance. Every show . . . came to rehearse in Harlem. Saturday, you walked down 7th Avenue and music was coming out of all the rehearsal halls. . . . Everywhere you went—you'd walk down between 140th and 141st Street. There's a band up there with the windows wide open. You heard the music. And I could just respond to music. . . . That was where I wanted to be."

The spirit of the Harlem Renaissance reached beyond New York to cities like Washington, D.C., and Chicago. It didn't matter where an African American lived. The important thing was to celebrate being black—to take pride in black history and culture, to be confident and self-reliant, to have self-respect, to expect fair treatment and equal rights as an American.

ABOVE LEFT James VanDerZee photographed this handsome and prosperous couple in Harlem in 1932. In the 1920s, with black migrants pouring in from the South and the Caribbean, Harlem became a center of cultural and intellectual excellence.

ABOVE RIGHT Thomas Wright Waller—who became known as Fats Waller—lived in New York City and started playing piano as a child. By 1922 he was performing and recording music. In 1923, he published his first composition, "Wild Cat Blues," and he continued to compose throughout his career. His piano-playing style influenced swing (a style of jazz music) pianists for generations to come.

William H. Johnson created this hand-colored woodcut titled *Evening* sometime in the 1930s. It portrays a father, a mother, and a baby in the mother's arms outside their house at sunset. Johnson moved from South Carolina to Harlem in 1918 and became an art student at the National Academy of Design in 1921. In 1929, he won a gold medal and a cash prize for his work in a prestigious national competition.

The Harlem Renaissance was not just cultural; it was also political. The NAACP kept the public informed about racial issues through its magazine, the *Crisis*, edited by W. E. B. Du Bois. It reached readers all over the country, even in the South, and was read and discussed in black communities. The National Urban League publication *Opportunity Journal*, edited by Charles S. Johnson, also championed justice for African Americans and was widely read. These organizations sponsored studies on job and housing discrimination and lynching. The NAACP held mass demonstrations. In 1917, three weeks after a race riot in East St. Louis, Illinois, that killed at least fifty people, ten thousand people marched under the NAACP banner in New York City, in silent protest of the event.

Discrimination and segregation were not only local issues but also national ones. Black activists realized this. The federal government itself practiced segregation beginning in 1913. The armed forces were segregated. Continued efforts to get Congress to pass a national anti-lynching law failed. When African Americans brought their demands to Washington, D.C., they almost always hit a wall. Their experiences raised questions about the commitment of the president of the United States, Congress, and the Supreme Court to ensure civil rights and to provide equal opportunities for all Americans.

TOP The NAACP held this protest parade in New York City in 1917 after a race riot in East St. Louis, Illinois. The riot shocked the country. African Americans were alarmed because the riot took place in a northern state, not in the South. It was a sign of the tension caused by growing numbers of black migrants who settled in northern, midwestern, and western cities.

BOTTOM From its beginnings in 1909, the NAACP fought for civil rights, an end to segregation, and a national anti-lynching law. In this photo, taken between 1930 and 1950 by M. Smith, NAACP members in Harlem pose. They are selling anti-lynching buttons to raise money for NAACP campaigns.

WHY SHOULD WE MARCH?

15,000 Negroes Assembled at St. Louis, Missouri
20,000 Negroes Assembled at Chicago, Illinois
23,500 Negroes Assembled at New York City
Millions of Negro Americans all Over This Great
Land Claim the Right to be Free!

FREE FROM WANT!
FREE FROM FEAR!
FREE FROM JIM CROW!

"Winning Democracy for the Negro is Winning the War for Democracy!" — A. Philip Randolph

Americans against segregation and discrimination were looking to the federal government for help when the proposal for the March on Washington surfaced in 1941. This flyer mentions the number of black Americans who had protested in various cities before, and it invites participants to come to the nation's capital and demand freedom from Jim Crow laws. A. Philip Randolph, a labor and civil rights leader, proposed the march.

THE
NATION

Relationships between black and white Americans have been a part of the story of the United States since its founding in 1776. The Declaration of Independence declares that "all men are created equal," but many of the signers of the declaration owned slaves. The U.S. Constitution, written in 1787, did not abolish slavery. Slavery was allowed in the nation's capital, Washington, D.C., until April 16, 1862—one year *after* the Civil War began. For a time after the war ended, Congress tried to protect the rights of the newly freed slaves by passing the Thirteenth, Fourteenth, and Fifteenth Amendments to the Constitution; continuing the Freedmen's Bureau; and stationing federal troops in the southern states. By the end of the 1870s, the federal government had virtually withdrawn its support for African American rights in the South, deciding that southern whites knew best how to manage their own states. It focused instead on national economic growth, expansion into the West, and building up trade and power internationally.

Still, African Americans continued to serve as U.S. soldiers—although in segregated units—and to have jobs in the federal government, where they were not, at first, segregated or discriminated against. In fact, the civil service, the part of government that provided men and women for office work in departments like the Postal Service and the Treasury Department, employed more African Americans—about 12,000—by 1912 than any other employer in the country.

By scoring well on a fair and unbiased civil service exam, African Americans were appointed to many federal jobs in the late nineteenth and early twentieth centuries. One federal worker was Daniel A. P. Murray, who became the personal assistant to the Librarian of Congress in 1871 and rose to become assistant librarian in ten years. Murray searched out and acquired a collection of nearly 1,500 books and other written materials by African Americans, which he donated to the Library of Congress in 1925.

Since the 1880s, the way to get civil service jobs was to score well on an exam, and black people did as well as white people on these exams.

But after Woodrow Wilson was elected president in 1912—with the votes of many black men, to whom he had promised "absolute fair dealing"—segregation became the practice in several government offices. In 1913, members of Wilson's cabinet—the postmaster general, secretary of the Treasury, and secretary of the Navy—began separating blacks and whites who had been working together. Partitions were built between white and black workers in offices and lunchrooms. Restrooms were segregated in, for example, the Government Printing Office. Some African Americans lost their jobs; others were demoted. President Wilson took away jobs that were traditionally held by black people, such as diplomatic minister to Haiti and register of the Treasury, and gave them to whites.

Introducing Jim Crow into the workings of the federal government resulted in strong opposition. In 1913 and 1914, the NAACP sponsored heavily attended mass meetings in such cities as Baltimore, Maryland; Takoma, Washington; Portland, Maine; and Washington, D.C. The National Independent Political League, founded by African American

William Monroe Trotter, distributed a petition in newspapers and through churches and meetings across the country that called for an end to federal Jim Crow. Twenty thousand people in thirty-six states signed the petition. It was presented to President Wilson by a group of African American leaders, including Trotter and the journalist Ida B. Wells.

Discriminatory practices continued, however. By 1914, people applying for civil service jobs had to submit a photograph in addition to passing an exam. Now those hiring could tell whether applicants were black or white before offering them a job, no matter how well they did on the exam. Trotter, with a group from the National Equal Rights League, met again with President Wilson in November 1914. Trotter directly challenged the president's position on segregation. Wilson defended the civil service changes as good for blacks as well as whites, because "the friction, or rather the discontent and uneasiness which had prevailed in many of the departments would thereby be removed." Wilson's comments, as well as Trotter's willingness to confront him, caused a national controversy. However, discrimination in the civil service continued until the presidency of Franklin D. Roosevelt (1933–45), when African Americans would again find jobs in the federal government.

Woodrow Wilson was still president when the United States entered World War I in April 1917. (The war began in Europe in 1914.) The army accepted a limited number of black men, then turned away others who wanted to enlist. A month later, Congress passed, and the president signed, a law to draft soldiers. The first African Americans were drafted in September. They were sent to training camps throughout the country and kept in segregated units. One camp in Des Moines, Iowa, was set up to train black officers; fourteen camps trained white officers.

By the time the war ended in 1918, approximately 380,000 black men had served. Only 20 percent took part in battles. An army report stated that "the mass of the colored drafted men cannot be used for combatant troops" but should "be organized in reserve labor battalions." They loaded and unloaded cargo from boats, did construction work, and maintained camp sites. Some black American soldiers were assigned to the French army, however, where they excelled. Three regiments of the U.S. Ninety-third Division were awarded France's Croix de Guerre (Cross of War) for bravery.

On the home front, many African Americans supported World War I. However, what Ellen Tarry of Birmingham, Alabama, remembered about the war was that "though we carried huge signs in the parade about fighting for democracy and how everybody should buy bonds, the Negro children were still put at the end of the procession."

When the composer Bill Broonzy arrived home in Arkansas after serving in World War I, he said, "I had a nice uniform . . . and I met a white fellow that was knowing me before I went in the army and so he told me, 'Listen, boy . . .

now you been in the army?' I told him, 'Yeah.' He says, 'How did you like it?' I said, 'It's okay.' He says, 'Well, you ain't in the army now. . . . And those clothes you got there . . . you can take [them] off and get you some overhalls [overalls], because there's no n_____'s gonna walk around here with no Uncle Sam's uniform on . . . up and down *these* streets.'"

Bill Broonzy was one of tens of thousands of black soldiers "welcomed" home by Jim Crow. They had experienced a world outside segregation, and they returned with more confidence and a determination not to be treated as second-class citizens. But many white people did not want the system of segregation to change. They were fearful of blacks who were ambitious and of those who did not follow the rigid rules about how blacks should behave toward whites. In 1919, the year after World War I ended, seventy-seven African Americans were lynched in the South, twenty of them U.S. Army veterans. Hundreds were beaten or forced to leave their homes. Racial riots broke out in Charleston, South Carolina; Washington, D.C.; and Knoxville, Tennessee. By the end of the year, riots had erupted in more than twenty-five cities, South and North.

OPPOSITE African American U.S. Army infantry troops march northwest of Verdun, France, on November 5, 1918, during World War I. Black men and women served in segregated military units during both World War I and World War II.

LEFT This flag—"A Man Was Lynched Yesterday"—was hung outside the NAACP offices at 69 Fifth Avenue in New York City to remind people of how often lynchings happened. The photograph was taken in 1936; in 1938, the threat of losing its lease forced the NAACP to stop flying the flag.

In the North, racial fears about the growing number of African Americans living there created conflict. World War I brought thousands of black migrants to northern cities—sixty thousand had moved to Chicago, for example, by the war's end. Suspicion and prejudice led to an anti-black riot there in August 1919 that lasted for thirteen days. An estimated thirty-eight people died, and thousands of black people lost their homes. Competition over jobs also built up tension. In September 1919, steelworkers went on strike throughout the North, including the states of Illinois, Pennsylvania, New York, Ohio, Colorado, and West Virginia. These workers were members of a union that did not accept African Americans. Thirty thousand black workers, who needed the jobs and were not protected by a union, replaced the white workers, who felt threatened and angry.

The Great Depression of the 1930s slowed the number of black migrants to the North. White people and black, North and South, suffered economically. Franklin Roosevelt, who took office as president of the United States in 1933, created new government agencies to provide relief to the unemployed, to repair the country's economy, and to offer jobs to those who were out of work. Roosevelt's program was called the New Deal, and it was meant to help all Americans. Roosevelt was sympathetic to the problems African Americans faced. He quietly ordered discrimination to end in federal employment. Between 1932 and 1940, the number of African Americans working for the federal government tripled, to nearly 150,000 people.

However, Roosevelt was limited in what he could do for black people by the power of southerners in Congress and by the prejudice and segregation in both the North and the South. Many of his programs, intended to help the worker, largely helped the *white* worker. Wages for farmers and domestic laborers, the two occupations of most African Americans, were not supervised or guided by federal programs. The Home Owners' Loan Corporation and the Federal Housing Administration aided home buyers in getting loans. But these groups almost always decided that "black" neighborhoods were not worthy of credit, so African Americans rarely got federal help with home loans and mortgages.

First Lady Eleanor Roosevelt opposed such racial discrimination. She was an outspoken champion of black civil rights. She persuaded her husband to appoint activist Mary McLeod Bethune, founder and president of the National Council of Negro Women, as an adviser to the federal government. Mrs. Roosevelt supported anti-lynching laws. In 1939, at a meeting of the Southern Conference for Human Welfare in Alabama, she discovered that the seating was segregated. She sat by herself in the aisle separating black and white delegates. That same year, the all-white Daughters of the American Revolution refused to allow the renowned African American opera singer Marian Anderson to perform in their building, Constitution Hall, in Washington, D.C. Mrs. Roosevelt resigned from the group and helped to arrange Anderson's appearance in an outdoor concert at the Lincoln Memorial. In 1945, she became a member of the NAACP's board of directors.

First Lady Eleanor Roosevelt presents the Spingarn Medal—the NAACP's highest honor—to singer Marian Anderson in 1939. Earlier that year, the all-white group Daughters of the American Revolution (DAR) refused to allow Anderson to perform in its hall in Washington, D.C., because she was African American. Mrs. Roosevelt resigned from the DAR, saying, "to remain a member implies approval of that action, and therefore I am resigning."

The NAACP, the National Urban League, and other activist groups continued to fight against discrimination. In 1939, the United States was coming out of the Great Depression. World War II had begun. Great Britain and France (the Allies) were fighting Germany and Italy (the Axis); and in Asia, Japan (Axis) and China (Ally) were at war. The United States did not enter the war then, but it did supply the Allied countries with arms and equipment. The United States also prepared itself, in case it was forced to go to war with the Axis countries. There was a need for more and more workers in the defense industries—those that made weapons, airplanes, and ships. Yet black men and women were not being hired for these jobs. For example, in 1940, of the 107,000 workers in the aircraft industry, only 240 were black.

The National Urban League held what it called a "monster protest demonstration" in Kansas City, Missouri, where six thousand blacks rallied. "National Defense Day" protests organized by branches of the NAACP took place in twenty-three cities in January 1941. On January 15, A. Philip Randolph, a nationally known labor and civil rights activist, issued a statement to newspapers, which was published throughout the country. "I suggest that TEN THOUSAND Negroes march on Washington, D.C. . . . with the slogan: 'WE LOYAL NEGRO AMERICAN CITIZENS DEMAND THE RIGHT TO WORK AND FIGHT FOR OUR COUNTRY.' . . . One thing is certain and that is if Negroes are going to get anything out of this national defense, which will cost the nation 30 or 40 billions of dollars that we Negroes must help pay for in taxes . . . WE MUST FIGHT FOR IT AND FIGHT FOR IT WITH GLOVES OFF." Randolph later upped the number to one hundred thousand people and scheduled the march for July. With NAACP president Walter White, he told President Roosevelt that all of these people would march in Washington, D.C., unless the government issued an order to end job discrimination. This became the March on Washington Movement.

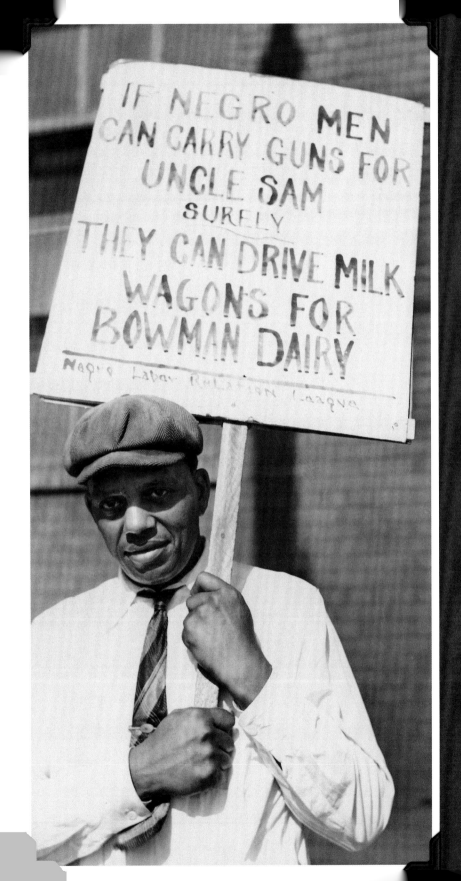

LEFT An African American man protests against job discrimination in Chicago in this 1941 photograph taken by John Vachon. His sign reads, "If Negro Men Can Carry Guns for Uncle Sam Surely They Can Drive Milk Wagons For Bowman Dairy."

ABOVE President Franklin Roosevelt issued Executive Order 8802 in 1941, banning discrimination in defense industries. These women welders are shown working at the Landers, Frary, and Clark aircraft plant in New Britain, Connecticut, in 1943, in a photograph taken by Gordon Parks. Roosevelt's order did not end discrimination, but it opened the way for more black women to have industrial jobs, especially as men were drafted into the military, causing a shortage of workers.

Concerned that a huge march would be politically embarrassing, Roosevelt issued Executive Order 8802 on June 24, 1941. It prohibited discrimination in hiring for the defense industry and the federal government, as well as in job training. Roosevelt also created the Fair Employment Practices Committee (FEPC) to enforce the order. The FEPC had a small staff and budget. It could not take on all the cases of job discrimination, but it did let Americans know about defense factories that discriminated, in the hope that they would be persuaded to hire black workers. Randolph called off the March on Washington.

When Japanese planes attacked the U.S. Navy base at Pearl Harbor on December 7, 1941, the United States joined the Allies to fight World War II. African Americans were determined to make World War II a different experience than World War I had been, but again they faced Jim Crow in the military. After Pearl Harbor, a teenage Pearle W. Mack Jr. tried to enlist in the U.S. Army at a federal building in Kansas. "Waiting in line with others, mostly white . . . the young men were called one-at-a-time," Mack said. "About noon the processing was finished, however I was still sitting alone on the now empty bench. . . . The recruiting officer and staff opened their office door and exclaimed, 'What are you waiting for?'. . . [I said,] 'I know what happened yesterday [Pearl Harbor] and I came to offer my service.' The officer . . . glared down at me and said, 'The army doesn't have a quota for n_____s.'"

Pearle Mack Jr. was finally accepted into the U.S. Army. During World War II, nearly a million black men and women served. White and black units were still segregated, however, and whites were largely in command. "Whenever one of us got a command in World War II, it was because they ran out of white guys to command the units," commented Isaiah A. McCoy Jr., a black soldier who eventually rose to the rank of colonel.

LEFT Tuskegee-trained pilot Edward C. Gleed stands in front of his airplane at the American base in Ramitelli, Italy, in 1945. This photograph was taken by Toni Frissell, one of several female photographers who covered World War II.

ABOVE Many African American soldiers were assigned to do construction and maintenance work during World War II, but others were in combat. These U.S. Marines are in a tank turret, prepared for battle, in 1943.

Although many African Americans were assigned to service units, where they handled construction, maintenance, and supply, they made some progress—through their own persistence—in experiencing combat. For example, some six hundred black pilots trained at Tuskegee Institute, in Alabama. Lee Archer, born in 1919 in Yonkers, New York, was one of them. As a child, he had spent summers in Saratoga, New York, near a small airfield. "I had made a decision that I wanted to fly . . . in World War II. . . . I didn't know about the rules and regulations which had decided that African Americans could never be in the Army Air Corps." He persisted in his ambition because of "an internal belief that you can't tell me I can't do something," he said. "I was willing to fight for the country, to die for the country, despite its faults, warts and all, that was it."

At the Tuskegee Institute in Alabama, African American men trained for the first time to be part of the Army Air Corps. In January 1942, these men are learning to send and receive Morse code. They are Captain Roy F. Morse, at the head of the table, with, at left (*front to back*), James B. Knighton, Lee Rayford, and C. H. Flowers Jr., and at right (*front to back*), George Levi Knox, Sherman W. White Jr., and Mac Ross.

Until 1945, the U.S. military services had a quota (a set number) for how many African Americans could serve as nurses. These nurses, photographed in 1944 by Frank Prist, were assigned to duty in Australia before the quota was lifted. They are, from left, Jean L. Hamilton, Geneva H. Culpepper, Marjorie S. Mayers, Prudence L. Burnes, and Inez F. Holmes.

Lee Archer was assigned to the Sixteenth Training Battalion at Camp Wheeler, in Macon, Georgia. "They put us on a train [in the North] along with a number of other African American troops, and we were all over the train till we got to Washington, D.C., the Capitol of my country that I was going to fight for, and they pulled us, all of the Colored troops, off the train and put us in the first car behind a coal driven engine and gave our seats to white people. . . . We got off the train in Macon, Georgia. They had two train station rooms, a big fancy one that had a sign over it that said, 'white,' and a little small section on the other side of it that said, 'Colored.'" Eventually, he trained as part of the Ninety-ninth Pursuit Squadron at Tuskegee. This squadron flew more than two hundred missions to escort bomber planes behind enemy lines and bring them back safely. Its record of success was excellent. The Tuskegee airmen as a group received three Distinguished Unit Citations for Action against the enemy. Eighty-two African American pilots were awarded the Distinguished Flying Cross.

Black women also served during World War II. The Women's Auxiliary Army Corps accepted African Americans; the navy, however, did not accept black women until October 1944, after steady protest against this discrimination. African American women were accepted as army nurses as early as 1940, but under a quota system. Again, there was protest, much of it from the National Association of Colored Graduate Nurses. The quota was lifted in January 1945, and applicants were accepted without regard to race. Black nurses, however, were assigned to care only for black soldiers, not white. (Sometimes they also nursed enemy prisoners of war.) Despite loyal service by nearly one million African American men and women in the armed services during World War II, segregation in the U.S. military did not end until 1948, three years *after* the war ended.

The treatment of black soldiers raised issues about the injustice of Jim Crow in dramatic ways. The United States proclaimed that it fought World War II to keep the world safe for democracy, so that people in all countries could have basic rights and fair governments. Why, then, did it take away the rights of African Americans and discriminate against them? Black people pointed out this contradiction during World War II by publicizing the idea of a "Double V" victory: victory against undemocratic countries overseas *and* victory against racial inequality at home. Articles in black-owned newspapers, rallies, and protests kept the Double V campaign in the public eye.

The March on Washington Movement had the same goals as the Double V campaign. Just as it fought discrimination in defense jobs, it continued to fight segregation of the U.S. military. A. Philip Randolph insisted on the "democratic rights of Negroes now, during the war." In June 1942, twenty-five thousand people demonstrated for civil rights in New York City's Madison Square Garden. In July, the demonstrators "kept a running fire of street meetings every night," according to Pauli Murray. She joined a "truckful of young radicals" who "skittered down 125th St. [in Harlem], shouting in jitterbug rhythm, 'HEY, JOE—WHADDYE KNOW—OLE JIM CROW—HAS GOT TO GO!'" In Detroit, on April 11, 1943, ten thousand people marched carrying signs that read, "DOWN WITH DISCRIMINATION," "JIM CROW MUST GO," and "BULLETS AND BOMBS ARE COLORBLIND." The protesters included African American soldiers and civil defense workers dressed in their uniforms.

In addition to large rallies, there were sit-ins and small demonstrations throughout the North in the 1940s. (Sit-ins at first took place at white-only restaurants, where protesters—black and white—sat at tables or the counter and requested service but were denied. They kept their seats, however,

Americans believed they were fighting World War II to preserve human rights and democratic government, but they denied rights to black Americans in the United States. Here, an African American soldier serving his country in the U.S. Army waits for a bus from Louisville, Kentucky, to Memphis, Tennessee, next to white travelers. When he boards the bus, he will have to ride in the back, in segregated seating.

occupying space that "acceptable" white customers could not use. Later sit-in locales included schools and other public places.) In 1942, James Farmer and George Houser began the organization that became the Congress of Racial Equality (CORE). Farmer was African American. When his father asked him what he planned to do after he graduated from college, he replied, "Destroy segregation." He was a civil rights leader for the rest of his life. Houser, who was white, had helped to organize and plan the March on Washington Movement.

CORE had many white members as well as black members. They were inspired by their Christian faith and believed in nonviolent protest. In Chicago the organization tried to convince two restaurants to integrate. These restaurants were rude to black customers, serving them spoiled food, some of it garbage.

ABOVE Civil rights demonstrations continued during World War II. In this 1942 photograph by Gordon Parks, Congressman Adam Clayton Powell from New York (*center*), with other African Americans, are in Washington, D.C., to protest a filibuster against a bill to abolish the poll tax for voters. During a filibuster, members of Congress keep talking for days and days, so that a bill can never come up for a vote. Southern congressmen used this tactic to keep bills they did not like—like one banning lynching—from being passed into law.

OPPOSITE On April 11, 1943, ten thousand civil rights protesters marched in Detroit, some of them soldiers and civil defense workers. A little more than two months later, on June 22, white mobs rioted against blacks there. This photo shows passengers climbing out of a streetcar stopped by a mob in Detroit. Race riots took place in nearly fifty American cities in 1943.

When polite requests to change segregated policies didn't work, they organized a sit-in at one restaurant and blocked the door at the other. Both protests were successful. Juanita Nelson, a CORE member in Cleveland, Ohio, believed that "all you had to do was get a few people to sit in a restaurant or stand in front of a theater box office" to attack segregation. "Public accommodations [were] easier than anything else to crack. . . . Job discrimination was harder to prove. How do you prove that somebody was qualified for a job[?]"

White segregationists resisted these efforts. Racial tension over jobs, housing, and civil rights did not decrease in the 1940s. In 1943, a total of 242 racial riots took place in forty-seven U.S. cities. Four of the worst were in Los Angeles; New York City (Harlem); Mobile, Alabama; and Detroit, Michigan. Some white people also declared that fighting for civil rights hurt the effort to win World War II, creating disunity in the United States and making the country weaker. Instead of granting civil rights, they proposed that all Americans accept segregation. "VICTORY DEMANDS YOUR COOPERATION," read a sign in a Charleston, South Carolina, bus. "IF THE PEOPLES OF THIS COUNTRY'S RACES DO NOT PULL TOGETHER, VICTORY IS LOST. WE, THEREFORE, RESPECTFULLY DIRECT YOUR ATTENTION TO THE LAWS AND CUSTOMS OF THE STATE IN REGARD TO SEGREGATION. YOUR COOPERATION IN CARRYING THEM OUT WILL MAKE THE WAR SHORTER AND VICTORY SOONER. AVOID FRICTION. BE PATRIOTIC. WHITE PASSENGERS WILL BE SEATED FROM FRONT TO REAR. COLORED PASSENGERS FROM REAR TO FRONT."

ONE OF
AMERICA'S
GREAT
NEWSPAPERS

NEW YORK
Amsterdam News

NATIONAL
EDITION

VOL. XXXVIII—NO. 20   SATURDAY, APRIL 19, 1947   Entered As Second Class Matter Post Office Bethlehem, Pa.   10c

MAJOR LEAGUER: Jackie Robinson of the National League's Brooklyn Dodgers.—Solomon Photo.

In 1947, Jackie Robinson became the first African American to play in the major leagues. Here he is on the front page of the April 19, 1947, issue of the *New York Amsterdam News*, an African American newspaper. Robinson was taunted and threatened by baseball fans and players, but he stayed in the game. At the end of the season, he was honored as Rookie of the Year.

After World War II, the days when segregation could be thought of as "patriotic" were also coming to an end—not completely, and not for another ten to twenty years, but cracks were forming in the system. The integration of major league baseball in the 1940s was one sign that the United States was changing. Professional baseball had been segregated for about seventy years. It followed the path that other forms of segregation took. When the National Association of Baseball Players was founded in 1857—while there was still slavery—no "persons of color" were allowed to play. In 1871, when the National Association of Professional Baseball Players was formed, during Reconstruction, African Americans did play on teams in this league. But in the 1880s, white owners began to eliminate blacks from their teams. By 1898—two years after the "separate but equal" decision—black teams were no longer playing against white teams. In the 1920s, the Negro National League was formed. Negro League games were very popular, drawing large crowds

In 1945, the year the war ended, Jackie Robinson, who played for a Negro League team, the Kansas City Monarchs, signed a contract with the all-white Brooklyn Dodgers. He played on their minor-league team, the Montreal Royals, in 1946 and then with the Dodgers in 1947. "Every stadium that year was a battleground," his wife, Rachel Robinson, said of his first year with the Dodgers. "From the start of the season, he felt he was a target. Some players—on opposing teams, and even on the Dodgers—threatened to strike if they had to join Jack on the field. There were deliberate efforts to physically hurt him. . . . By midseason threatening letters began to arrive in the mail." Branch Rickey, the white president and general manager of the Dodgers who had signed Robinson, also faced great opposition and hostile reactions from other managers, players, umpires, fans, and the news media. But Robinson was a great ballplayer, and he persisted. In 1955, he received this telegram from Jim Vance, a fan from Texas: "JUST SAW YOU STEAL HOME ON TV GREAT FROM A 50 YEAR OLD DEEP SOUTH WHITE MAN I SAY YOU ARE THE FINEST AND A GENTLEMAN."

The same year that Robinson integrated baseball, CORE sponsored a "Journey of Reconciliation," sending eight black and eight white men on a bus trip through Virginia, North Carolina, Tennessee, and Kentucky. They were testing the 1946 Supreme Court decision in *Morgan v. Virginia* that said it was illegal to segregate bus passengers who were traveling from one state to another. They wanted to show that states in the South were not enforcing this decision but continued to segregate passengers by race. "Each day we would decide on two guinea pigs, a black [person] and a white [person] would sit together in the front or two whites would sit in the back, or two blacks would sit in the front," said Igal Roodenko, a white rider who participated.

Some bus drivers ignored where people were seated and drove on; others had the black and white riders arrested. They were arrested based on local and state laws still in effect in spite of the Supreme Court decision. Four of them were arrested in Chapel Hill, North Carolina—two whites and two African Americans. Igal Roodenko was one of those convicted and forced to work in a chain gang (prisoners chained together to work outside a prison)—and even the chain gangs were segregated. Yet he thought that other passengers "started responding" to the message of the Journey of Reconciliation. "People felt that . . . the [local and state] law was wrong and that discrimination against blacks was wrong."

Cracks in segregated education were also appearing in the late 1940s. The NAACP's Legal Defense and Educational Fund continued to fight segregation

The Congress of Racial Equality organized the "Journey of Reconciliation" in 1947 to test whether the southern states were following a federal order to allow black and white people to sit together on buses that went through more than one state. These "freedom riders" are ready to start their journey in Richmond, Virginia. They are from left, Worth Randle, Wally Nelson, Ernest Bromley, Jim Peck, Igal Roodenko, Bayard Rustin, Joe Felmet, George Houser, and Andy Johnson.

laws that applied to schools. It was hoping that challenges to these laws would reach the Supreme Court, which had the power to declare segregation unconstitutional. Thurgood Marshall headed the group. Marshall had already worked with Charles Houston, head of the NAACP's legal division, in the 1930s. They represented African Americans who were being turned down by all-white graduate or professional programs, such as law schools and medical schools. They argued that under *Plessy v. Ferguson*, states were required to provide *equal* schools for blacks and whites. Yet many states did not even have *separate* professional schools for black people or enough money to create them if required to do so by a court decision.

The fight for equality in education took place in middle schools and high schools as well as colleges. These students from Norfolk, Virginia, hold signs protesting unfair treatment of African American teachers by the local school board. This photo was taken in June 1939.

The NAACP won admission for a black student to the all-white University of Maryland Law School in 1936 and to the all-white University of Missouri School of Law in 1938 because the states could not provide a good alternative. In 1948, George McLaurin was turned down by the University of Oklahoma. He already had a master's degree in education and wanted to study for a doctorate. He took his case to court in Oklahoma, and the court decided that the university had to admit him. But the university made him sit by himself at a table in the cafeteria, and in class his desk was separate from those of the rest of the students. McLaurin returned to the Oklahoma court in 1949 to ask that the university stop this segregation. The court ruled against him. The NAACP took the case to the Supreme Court in 1950. In *McLaurin v. Oklahoma*, the Supreme Court decided that the university was denying McLaurin his rights under the Fourteenth Amendment and had to allow him the same treatment as the white students received.

McLaurin v. Oklahoma was a step in the right direction. The NAACP knew it would lose some cases in the state courts, but it still hoped for a decision by the Supreme Court that would declare that *all* segregation laws

As African Americans demonstrated against segregated schools, many white parents and students took part in demonstrations protesting integration. This group stands in front of Rock Junior High School in Little Rock, Arkansas, sometime around 1950. They did not want the school to accept black students. One of the signs reads, "The Negros—If They Stay—We Go."

went against the Fourteenth Amendment of the Constitution. Separate desks and tables at the University of Oklahoma did not make them equal. Here was a branch of the federal government—the Supreme Court—supporting the rights of African Americans over the states. It had been the federal government that allowed black people to have some rights in the nineteenth century. Now it was signaling that it might take an active role in protecting civil rights again.

After *McLaurin v. Oklahoma*, the NAACP was ready to tackle segregation in elementary and high schools. In 1949, seventeen states and the city of Washington, D.C., still had laws requiring segregated elementary and high schools for black and white children. Most of these were the southern and border states: Alabama, Arkansas, Florida, Georgia, Kentucky, Louisiana, Mississippi, Missouri, North Carolina, Oklahoma, South Carolina, Tennessee, Texas, and West Virginia. Three were in the North: Connecticut, Massachusetts, and Rhode Island. Four states—Arizona, Kansas, New Mexico, and Wyoming—did not order segregation for every school but allowed each school district to decide whether it wanted separate schools.

In 1950 and 1951, the NAACP and parents of students sued school districts in four of these states and the District of Columbia. These parents wanted their children to attend the white schools, which had far better buildings and resources than the black ones. They were not the first to challenge segregation in high school or grade school; the first case came up in 1849 in Boston. But these five cases were heard before state courts and eventually brought before the Supreme Court, as intended by the NAACP, when the state courts ruled against the challengers. The cases were considered under one name: *Oliver Brown et al. v. Board of Education of Topeka, Kansas.*

The five cases were *Briggs v. Elliot*; *Brown v. Board of Education of Topeka, Kansas*; *Belton v. Gebhart* (paired with *Bulah v. Gebhart* as one case); *Davis v. County School Board of Prince Edward County, Virginia*; and *Bolling v. C. Melvin Sharpe.* Each of these cases told the story of individual communities and situations, but they all had one thing in common: African Americans living under Jim Crow.

In 1951, the first of these cases began. Twenty black parents in Clarendon County, South Carolina, joined with the NAACP to sue against the inferior conditions of the schools provided for their children. They signed a petition objecting to the poor quality of the buildings, the lack of transportation, and the teachers' salaries, which were lower than salaries for whites. The case took its name from one of the parents, Harry Briggs Sr.: *Briggs v. Elliot.* Liza Briggs, Harry Briggs's wife, and other women involved in the case were told by their employer, the Summerton Motel, to "take [their] names off the petition in order to work." Liza Briggs would not. "I didn't want to do that because we would be hurting the children, and I'd rather give up my job. . . . So in about two weeks' time I was fired. Not only me, the rest of them who had anything to do with

LEFT In the early 1950s, black parents and the NAACP were active in suing school districts to end segregation. They were protesting conditions like those depicted in this photo, taken in 1934 in Pleasant Grove, South Carolina. It shows rows of African American students sitting in threes on seats that were only thirty-six inches wide.

BELOW This bus took African American students back and forth to school in Louisa County, Virginia, in 1935. The NAACP used such photos as these to support its claim that black children were not treated fairly where schools were segregated.

the petition." R. W. Elliott, the defendant named in the case, was the chairman of the Clarendon County Board of Trustees of Summerton High School. Six other board members were also defendants. The NAACP lost the case in South Carolina.

Oliver Brown gave his name to the next case, one that involved his daughter Linda, *Brown v. Board of Education of Topeka, Kansas*. She and nineteen other black children were turned away from white schools in Topeka, even though many of them lived closer to the white schools than to the black schools. Linda Brown, who was seven, had to cross dangerous railroad tracks and ride on a run-down bus to get to school. They sued the defendant, Topeka's board of education. The NAACP lawyers lost this case in a Kansas court.

The third case in *Brown v. Board of Education* involved African American high school students in Claymont, Delaware. They had to ride a bus for almost an hour to go to the one black high school in Wilmington. Other Delaware students, in Hockessin, were made to attend a run-down, one-room school. Again, their parents sued—two of the mothers, Ethel Belton and Shirley Bulah, gave their names to these cases: *Belton v. Gebhart* and *Bulah v. Gebhart*. Francis Gebhart, the named defendant, was a member of the Delaware State Board of Education. The state supreme court of Delaware agreed with the parents and ruled in their favor. But its decision affected only the Claymont and Hockessin students, not all the African American students and schools in Delaware.

Another case that became part of *Brown v. Board of Education* was begun by a sixteen-year-old, Barbara Johns. She called a student strike at the Robert Russa Moton High School in Prince Edward County, Virginia. Her sister, Joan Johns Cobb, a freshman at the time, remembered, "The school . . . was overcrowded. Consequently, the county decided to build three tarpaper shacks for us to hold classes in. A tarpaper shack . . . is similar to a chicken coop on a farm. . . . When it rained, we would get water through the ceiling [of the main school building]. So there were lots of pails sitting around the classroom. . . . And sometimes we had to raise our umbrellas to keep the water off our heads."

The students stayed out of the school, and Barbara Johns persuaded the NAACP to take on the case. "She was very persistent," said her sister. "She told [the NAACP lawyer] that we needed him and that he just had to come." Threatened with violence, Johns left Virginia, but the NAACP brought the case to court. It was named *Davis v. County School Board of Prince Edward County, Virginia*, after Dorothy Davis, a fourteen-year-old ninth grader who attended Moton High School. The Prince Edward County School Board was the defendant. The Virginia court said that the school district had to provide equal facilities for the black students. They were not, however, allowed to attend the white schools.

One more case was considered by the Supreme Court at the same time that the judges made their decision about the other schools in *Brown v. Board of Education*. When eleven African American students were denied admittance to a new and well-built junior high school in Washington, D.C., their parents and the NAACP sued. The case, *Bolling v. C. Melvin Sharpe*, took its name from one of the students, twelve-year-old Spottswood Bolling. The defendant, C. Melvin Sharpe, was the acting president of the District of Columbia Board of Education. The Fourteenth Amendment protected

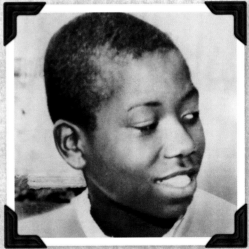

Spottswood Bolling was one of the black students not allowed to attend a new middle school for white students in Washington, D.C. His name was on the case *Bolling v. C. Melvin Sharpe*, one of the five cases in *Brown v. Board of Education*. This photo was taken on May 18, 1954, one day after the Supreme Court announced its decision.

only citizens of states like Delaware, Kansas, South Carolina, and Virginia, however. It did not protect people living in the District of Columbia, which was not (and still is not) a state. So the Supreme Court issued a separate decision in the case of *Bolling v. Sharpe* even though it was heard with the other four cases.

On May 17, 1954, the court decided in *Brown v. Board of Education* that school segregation was unconstitutional. All nine justices, three of whom were from southern states, agreed. Their decision stated that "segregation of white and colored children in public schools has a detrimental [damaging] effect upon the colored children. The impact is greater when it has the sanction [approval] of the law, for the policy of separating the races is usually interpreted as denoting the inferiority of the negro group. . . . In these days, it is doubtful that any child may reasonably be expected to succeed in life if he is denied the opportunity of an education. Such an opportunity . . . is a right which must be made available to all on equal terms. We come to the questions presented: Does segregation of children in public schools solely on the basis of race, even though the physical facilities . . . may be equal, deprive the children of the minority group of equal educational opportunities? We believe that it does."

The *Washington Post* called the *Brown* decision "a new birth of freedom." While many African Americans were hopeful, they were not willing to go that far. After all, they had won court decisions against segregation and discrimination before, and those decisions had not been enforced. In fact, schools were *not* immediately integrated after *Brown*. State governments, local school districts, and white parents tried to keep schools segregated. This became one of the great battles of the civil rights movement of the 1950s and 1960s, especially in the South. Even today, schools can be segregated because African Americans and white people still live in largely segregated neighborhoods.

Like the Supreme Court judges in *Plessy v. Ferguson*, the judges who decided the *Brown v. Board of Education* case were all white men. The *Brown* judges, shown in this December 1953 photograph, were (*front row, from left*) Felix Frankfurter, Hugo Black, Chief Justice Earl Warren, Stanley Reed, William O. Douglas, and (*back row, from left*) Tom Clark, Robert H. Jackson, Harold Burton, and Sherman Minton. But unlike the *Plessy* judges, these judges decided that separate was not equal and that school segregation was unconstitutional.

But in its legal implications and symbolic meaning, the *Brown* decision was momentous. It rejected the *Plessy* decision that had justified segregation for decades. "Where a State has undertaken to provide an opportunity for an education in its public schools, such an opportunity is a right which must be made available to all on equal terms." The federal government was again proclaiming civil rights for every American. No longer would "separate but equal" accommodations be considered legal. This was not a gift or a kindness on the part of the Supreme Court. It was a reminder that the *rights* granted in the Fourteenth Amendment were at the foundation of democracy and in the spirit and letter of the Constitution.

Some white people did not want integrated schools, no matter what the Supreme Court said. They protested outside school buildings and harassed black students. Here, National Guard troops safely escort a black student leaving a newly integrated school to a waiting car in Sturgis, Kentucky, in 1956. Other black students had to leave by the school's back door after classes to

There were also white parents and students who accepted school integration without making a fuss. Here, white and black children at the Barnard School in Washington, D.C., line up in their classroom on May 27, 1955.

Brown v. Board of Education opened the way for other kinds of segregation—in buses, restaurants, and theaters, for example—to be declared illegal. Clashes over civil rights would follow for twenty years or more, but the United States would never again accept without question the rightness of segregation. To reflect on the years before *Brown*—the years of rigid separation, widespread discrimination, cruel prejudice, and daily humiliation—is to understand how far the country had come in beginning to live up to its promise of equality for all. Those who endured injustice and those who never stopped fighting for fairness and opportunity placed their faith and their hope in the future that *Brown* brought closer. The civil rights movement that followed brought it closer still. In remembering this legacy, we ensure that the United States is a place where everyone can live with self-respect, dignity, and freedom.

TIME LINE

1890
- A state constitutional convention in Mississippi agrees to an amendment that would disqualify men from voting if they could not pass a literacy test or pay a poll tax.

1892
- The Populist Party, mostly made up of farmers, seeks support from African Americans in the South. Eventually, it will not welcome support from blacks.
- Homer Plessy is arrested for refusing to sit in the blacks-only car of a Louisiana train.

1895
- Booker T. Washington gives his "Atlanta Compromise" speech. He asks white people to allow African Americans to advance economically and in technical education. He does not ask for political or social equality.

1896
- The Supreme Court upholds the segregation of train cars in the decision *Plessy v. Ferguson*. The idea of "separate but equal" public facilities is based on this decision.
- The National Association of Colored Women is founded.

1898
- In *Williams v. Mississippi*, the Supreme Court declares that Mississippi can keep its literacy and poll-tax requirements for voting.

1900
- The National Negro Business League is founded in Boston after a meeting of black business people called by Booker T. Washington.
- A race riot in New Orleans, Louisiana, destroys black homes and schools.

1901
- George H. White of North Carolina finishes his term in the U.S. House of Representatives. He is the last African American to serve until Oscar De Priest is elected in 1928 in Illinois.

1903
- W. E. B. Du Bois publishes *The Souls of Black Folk*, a collection of essays arguing for civil rights for African Americans.

1905
- W. E. B. Du Bois, William Monroe Trotter, and other activist African Americans meet in Niagara Falls, New York, to discuss ways to achieve black equality. They begin the Niagara Movement.
- Robert S. Abbott publishes the first issue of the *Chicago Defender*, an influential activist black newspaper. The *Defender* encourages African Americans in the South to migrate north.

1906
- A race riot in Atlanta, Georgia, begins on September 22 and lasts for three or four days. Two white people and ten African Americans are confirmed dead, though estimates go as high as 25–40 deaths.

1908
- A race riot in Springfield, Illinois—near the home of President Abraham Lincoln—leads to a conference that results in the founding of the National Association for the Advancement of Colored People (NAACP).

1909
- The NAACP is established. It will be the most important civil rights organization in the United States for many years.
- James H. Anderson begins publishing the *Amsterdam News*, a black newspaper, in New York City.

1910
- The Committee on Urban Conditions Among Negroes (which will become the National Urban League) is founded to aid African Americans from the South who have migrated to the North.
- The NAACP magazine *Crisis* begins publication with W. E. B. Du Bois as editor.

1913
- Woodrow Wilson becomes president of the United States. His administration will institute segregation in some federal government offices.

1915
- In *Guinn v. United States*, the Supreme Court rules that using "grandfather clauses" to keep black people from voting is illegal. Grandfather clauses said that only men whose ancestors could vote as of January 1, 1867—a time when black men in the South were not qualified to vote—were allowed to cast a ballot.

1916
- Marcus Garvey organizes a New York chapter of the Universal Negro Improvement and Conservation Association and African Communities League (which later becomes the Univeral Negro Improvement Association). Chapters soon spring up throughout the country.

1917
- The United States enters World War I. Some 300,000 African Americans will serve in segregated units.
- Military force is needed to stop a race riot in East St. Louis, Illinois. A little more than three weeks later, 10,000 African Americans march silently in New York City to protest racial violence and discrimination.
- In *Buchanan v. Warley*, the Supreme Court says that laws that restrict African Americans from living in certain areas are illegal.

1919
- Race riots break out in more than twenty-five cities, including Washington, D.C., and Chicago, Illinois.
- In *State v. Young*, the Supreme Court rules that African Americans should be allowed to sit on juries.

1921
- A race riot in Tulsa, Oklahoma, on May 31 and June 1 destroys African American homes and businesses.

1922
- *The Book of American Negro Poetry*, edited by James Weldon Johnson, is published, calling attention to African American poetry.

1925
- *The New Negro*, edited by Alain Locke, is published. It showcases the cultural accomplishments of African Americans.
- A. Philip Randolph establishes the Brotherhood of Sleeping Car Porters, a pioneering union of black workers.

1927
- In *Nixon v. Herndon*, the Supreme Court rules that a Texas law that keeps black people from voting in primary elections is illegal.

1928
- Oscar De Priest is elected to the U.S. Congress from Illinois. He is the first black congressman elected in the twentieth century. He serves from 1929 to 1935.

1929
- The New York Stock Exchange crashes, one of the first signs of the Great Depression, which affects Americans throughout the 1930s.

1932
- Franklin Roosevelt is elected president of the United States during the Great Depression. He institutes a "New Deal" program to help Americans struggling with poverty and unemployment.

1936
- President Roosevelt appoints Mary McLeod Bethune director of the Division of Negro Affairs of the National Youth Administration.

1937
- In *Breedlove v. Suttles*, the Supreme Court rules that poll taxes are legal.

1938
- The Supreme Court decides, in *Gaines v. Canada*, that states must provide equal educational facilities for African Americans even if they are separate. This becomes one of the cases the NAACP uses to attack segregated education.

1939
- African American singer Marian Anderson performs at the Lincoln Memorial in Washington, D.C., after the Daughters of the American Revolution refuse to allow her to perform in their building, Constitution Hall.

1940
- Benjamin O. Davis Sr. is appointed brigadier general in the U.S. Army, becoming the highest-ranking black officer in the American military.

1941
- President Franklin Roosevelt issues Executive Order 8802, prohibiting discrimination in hiring for defense industries and in government training programs. He establishes the Fair Employment Practices Committee to watch out for discrimination.

- The United States enters World War II.

- The U.S. Army sets up a training school for African American pilots in Tuskegee, Alabama.

1942
- The Congress of Racial Equality (CORE) is formed by black and white activists in Chicago. CORE members take part in nonviolent protests such as sit-ins.

1943
- Race riots break out in several cities, including Los Angeles; New York City; Mobile, Alabama; and Detroit.

1944
- The Supreme Court rules that the "white primary"—in which only white people could vote in Democratic or Republican Party elections—is illegal in *Smith v. Allwright*.

1945
- World War II ends.

- More than a thousand white students walk out of classes in Gary, Indiana, to protest the integration of schools.

- Jackie Robinson signs a contract to play with the Brooklyn Dodgers. He plays on their minor-league team, the Montreal Royals, in 1946 and joins the Dodgers the following year.

1946
- In *Morgan v. Virginia*, the Supreme Court declares that it is illegal to segregate blacks and whites on buses that travel between two or more states.

- Harry Truman forms the President's Committee on Civil Rights. It issues a report, *To Secure These Rights*, in 1947, calling for an end to segregation.

1947
- CORE sends black and white "Freedom Riders" on a "Journey of Reconciliation" to test whether the Supreme Court's 1946 decision banning segregation on interstate bus travel is being enforced in the South. It is not, and Freedom Riders often face violence.

1948
- President Truman issues Executive Order 9981, which calls for an end to segregation in the military. The last all-black army unit shuts down in 1951.

- In *Sipuel v. University of Oklahoma*, the Supreme Court rules that Oklahoma must provide a law school for African Americans since there is one for white students in the state.

- In *Shelley v. Kraemer*, the Supreme Court rules that courts cannot be used to uphold restrictive housing covenants.

1950
- In *McLaurin v. Oklahoma*, the Supreme Court declares that a student cannot be segregated within a university once he or she has been admitted.

1951
- A race riot in Cicero, Illinois, takes place when an African American family attempts to move into an all-white neighborhood.

1952
- The Tuskegee Institute, which had kept track of lynchings for seventy-one years, reports that no recorded lynchings took place in 1952.

1953
- In *District of Columbia v. John R. Thompson Co.*, the Supreme Court rules that restaurants in Washington, D.C., cannot refuse service to African Americans.

- African Americans boycott the buses in Baton Rouge, Louisiana, to protest discriminatory treatment. After the boycott is called off, the city agrees to open seating on buses, except for the first two seats (saved for whites) and the last two seats (saved for blacks).

1954
- The Supreme Court rules in *Brown v. Board of Education* of Topeka, Kansas, that racial segregation in public schools is unconstitutional.

NOTES

Page vii: "At fifteen . . . back seat of the electric car." Albon Holsey, quoted in Leon F. Litwack, *Trouble in Mind: Black Southerners in the Age of Jim Crow* (New York: Knopf, 1998), p. 16.

Page ix: "founded in the color . . . race by color." Henry Billings Brown, quoted in *The Age of Jim Crow*, ed. Jane Dailey (New York: W. W. Norton, 2009), p. 71.

Page ix: "segregation . . . basis of race." FindLaw, http:laws.findlaw.com/us/347/483.html (accessed January 10, 2011).

Page 1: "I remember . . . through the hole." Charles Epps, quoted in Casey King and Linda Barrett Osborne, *Oh, Freedom! Kids Talk About the Civil Rights Movement with the People Who Made It Happen* (New York: Knopf, 1997), p. 12.

Page 2: On states with and without segregation laws and with anti-discrimination laws, shown on map. Edwin S. Newman, *The Law of Civil Rights and Civil Liberties* (New York: Oceana Publications, 1949), pp. 40–41.

Page 3: "I can remember . . . challenge white people." Charles Gratton, quoted in *Remembering Jim Crow: African Americans Tell About Life in the Segregated South*, eds. William H. Chafe, Raymond Gavins, and Robert Korstad (New York: New Press, 2001), p. 7.

Page 3: "It shall be unlawful . . . seven feet or higher." Birmingham, Alabama, city code, footnote 4, FindLaw, http://laws.findlaw.com/us/373/244.html (accessed September 9, 2010).

Page 4: "The partition . . . a fine of ten dollars." Durham, North Carolina, city code, quoted in LeMarquis DeJarmon, "Public Accommodations," *University of Illinois Law Forum*, no. 2, summer 1968, p. 189, footnote 2, http://heinonline.org/HOL/Page?handle=hein.journals/unillr1968&div=18&g_sent=1&collection=journals (accessed November 18, 2010).

Page 4: "It shall be unlawful . . . the white race." Georgia law, quoted in "Examples of Jim Crow Laws," *Jackson (Tennessee) Sun*, www.ferris.edu/jimcrow/links/misclink/examples (accessed September 9, 2010).

Page 4: "unlawful for a Negro . . . basketball or similar games." Birmingham, Alabama, city ordinance, University of Virginia, Amerian Studies, http://xroads.virginia.edu/~public/civilrights/ordinances.html (accessed September 9, 2010).

Page 4: "From the time . . . been that way." Leonard Barrow Jr., quoted in *Remembering Jim Crow*, eds. Chafe et al., p. 320.

Page 9: On the number of black men elected to office. C. Vann Woodward, *The Strange Career of Jim Crow* (New York: Oxford University Press, 2002), p. 54.

Page 9: "Uncle Richard Fitzgerald . . . appeared in North Carolina." Pauli Murray, *Proud Shoes: The Story of an American Family* (Boston: Beacon Press, 1999), p. 267.

Page 11: On black men voting in the South. *The Age of Jim Crow*, ed. Dailey, pp. xxv–xxvi.

Page 11: On the 1890 census. Campbell Gibson and Kay Jung, "Historical Census Statistics on Population Totals by Race, 1790 to 1990 . . .," at http://www.census.gov/population/www/documentation/twps0056/twps0056.html (accessed April 14, 2011). See tables for states and District of Columbia.

Page 12: "We seem as a race . . . this changed condition." *The Age of Jim Crow*, ed. Dailey, p. xv.

Page 15: On Homer Plessy. Keith Weldon Medley, *We As Freemen: Plessy v. Ferguson* (Gretna, LA: Pelican Publishing, 2003).

Page 15: On African Americans in the Louisiana legislature. Woodward, *Strange Career*, p. 54.

Page 16: "replied that he was a colored man." Medley, *We As Freemen*, p. 146.

Page 16: "founded in the color . . . race by color." Henry Billings Brown, quoted in *Age of Jim Crow*, ed. Dailey, p. 71.

Page 17: "the enforced separation . . . badge of inferiority." Ibid., p. 75.

Page 18: "The constitution . . . rights." John Marshall Holland, quoted in ibid., p. 77.

Page 18: "The common government . . . white citizens." Ibid., p. 81.

Page 18: "separate cars . . . certain nationalities." Henry Billings Brown, quoted in ibid., p. 74.

Page 18: "enact laws requiring . . . men's black." Ibid.

Page 18: On segregated transportation laws. Woodward, *Strange Career*, p. 97.

Page 19: On 1905 Georgia law. "Jim Crow Laws: Georgia," History of Jim Crow, http://www.jimcrowhistory.org/scripts/jimcrow/insidesouth.cgi?state=Georgia (accessed April 16, 2010).

Page 19: On Mobile, Alabama, law. Woodward, *Strange Career*, p. 101.

Page 20: On South Carolina law. Ibid., p. 98.

Page 20: On Mississippi and Washington, D.C., laws. *Age of Jim Crow*, ed. Dailey, p. xiv.

Page 20: On Louisiana law. Woodward, *Strange Career*, p. 99.

Page 20: On Oklahoma law. Oklahoma Historical Society, "Encyclopedia of Oklahoma History and Culture," http://digital.library.okstate.edu/encyclopedia/entries/S/SE006.html (accessed September 15, 2010).

Page 21: "Weel about . . . jump Jim Crow." Song lyrics at Ferris State University, Museum of Racist Memorabilia, http://www.ferris.edu/news/jimcrow/who.htm (accessed March 16, 2010).

Page 21: On lynching statistics. *Age of Jim Crow*, ed. Dailey, p. xxxix.

Page 22: "John Henry Corniggins . . . on his face." Murray, *Proud Shoes*, p. 262.

Page 22: "In many places . . . going to hush-hush." African American woman named Joanne, quoted in Raphael S. Ezekiel, *Voices from the Corner: Poverty and Racism in the Inner City* (Philadelphia: Temple University Press, 1984), p. 148.

Page 24: "[We] had to act . . . born and raised into." Ned Cobb, quoted in Litwack, *Trouble in Mind*, p. 3.

Page 26: "We automatically [knew] . . . the front porch off." Cleaster Mitchell, quoted in *Remembering Jim Crow*, eds. Chafe et al., p. 212.

Page 26: "I didn't understand . . . in the same store." Lillian Smith, quoted in ibid., p. 6.

Page 26: "Colored waiting rooms . . . in the bright lights." David Matthews, quoted in ibid., p. 108.

Page 27: "White men . . . blacks that way." Kenneth Young, quoted in ibid., p. 180.

Page 27: On Eloise Blake's arrest. Jennifer Rittenhouse, *Growing Up Jim Crow: How Black and White Southern Children Learned Race* (Chapel Hill: University of North Carolina Press, 2006), p. 46.

Page 27: "During my first year . . . hands off her." John Hope Franklin, *Mirror to America: The Autobiography of John Hope Franklin* (New York: Farrar, Straus and Giroux, 2005), p. 27.

Page 28: "You are as good as anybody!" Benjamin Mays, quoted in Litwack, *Trouble in Mind*, p. 25.

Page 29: "white people . . . thought they were." Charles Evers, quoted in ibid., p. 25.

Page 29: "would call me . . . That's my name.'" Olivia Cherry, quoted in *Remembering Jim Crow*, eds. Chafe et al., p. 314.

Page 29: "I carried on my own . . . 'peanut gallery.'" Pauli Murray, *The Autobiography of a Black Activist, Feminist, Lawyer, Priest, and Poet* (Knoxville: University of Tennessee Press, 1989), p. 32.

Page 29: On school funding. *Remembering Jim Crow*, eds. Chafe et al., p. 153.

Page 31: "I was six . . . passed on to us." William J. Croker, quoted in ibid., pp. 157–158.

Page 31: "I went to Chehaw elementary . . . go to the field." Ann Pointer, quoted in ibid., p. 55.

Page 32: "At I. C. Norcom . . . slipped it in." John W. Brown, quoted in ibid., p. 165.

Page 32: "things that you didn't . . . 'black history.'" Mamie Garvin Fields, quoted in Litwack, *Trouble in Mind*, p. 72.

Page 32: "My grandfather bought . . . not doing it then." Interview with Sarah Lee Anderson, 2004, National Visionary Leadership Project, housed in the Library of

Congress American Folklife Center. NVLP transcript file Anderson_Sarah.doc, p. 11. Used with permission of the NVLP.

Page 33: "a strong community . . . accounts for our strengths." Interview with Asa Hilliard, 2004, National Visionary Leadership Project, housed in the Library of Congress American Folklife Center. NVLP transcript file Hilliard_Asa.doc, pp. 6–7. Used with permission of the NVLP.

Page 34: "[T]here were things . . . on that machine." Leon Alexander, quoted in *Remembering Jim Crow*, eds. Chafe et al., p. 229.

Page 34: "I had applied . . . over forty years." John W. Brown, quoted in ibid., p. 167.

Page 37: "I seen that education . . . my accounts." Timothy Smith, quoted in Litwack, *Trouble in Mind*, p. 55.

Page 37: "The way I . . . let me rise." Ned Cobb, quoted in ibid., p. 123.

Page 37: "My parents . . . outside of a log." Walter M. Cavers, quoted in *Remembering Jim Crow*, eds. Chafe et al., p. 31.

Page 38: "We have a railroad . . . in another world." George Butterfield Jr., quoted in ibid., p. 131.

Page 38: "hardly more . . . 'Cripple Creek.'" James Robinson, quoted in Litwack, *Trouble in Mind*, p. 336.

Page 38: On the Atlanta death rate. Ibid., p. 337.

Page 38: "If you [were] a farmer . . . another mule." A. I. Dixie, quoted in *Remembering Jim Crow*, eds. Chafe et al., p. 90.

Page 41: "My father died . . . to look upward." Interview with Dovey Roundtree, February 22, 2003, National Visionary Leadership Project, housed in the Library of Congress American Folklife Center. NVLP transcript file DoveyRoundtree4loc.doc, p. 6. Used with permission of the NVLP.

Page 42: "one of the most . . . in my life." Maggie Dulin, quoted in *Remembering Jim Crow*, eds. Chafe et al., p. 95.

Page 43: On violence toward car owners. Litwack, *Trouble in Mind*, p. 335.

Page 43: "In the old, old days . . . the local black café." George Butterfield Jr., quoted in *Remembering Jim Crow*, eds. Chafe et al., pp. 130–31.

Page 43: "That's when I got . . . white motel." Irene Monroe, quoted in ibid., p. 139.

Page 46: "The building where . . . place of business stood." Buck Colbert Franklin, *My Life and Era: The Autobiography of Buck Colbert Franklin*, eds. John Hope Franklin and John Whittington Franklin (Baton Rouge: Louisiana State University Press, 1997), p. 197.

Page 47: "If my own city . . . self-assertive black man." W. E. B. Du Bois, quoted in Leon F. Litwack, *How Free Is Free? The Long Death of Jim Crow* (Cambridge, MA: Harvard University Press, 2009), p. 29.

Page 48: "Everything here . . . anywhere else." An African American resident of Mound Bayou, quoted in Litwack, *Trouble in Mind*, p. 376.

Page 51: "There were no signs . . . signs were present." Anna Arnold Hedgeman, quoted in Thomas J. Sugrue, *Sweet Land of Liberty: The Forgotten Struggle for Civil Rights in the North* (New York: Random House, 2008), p. 12.

Page 51: On Springfield, Ohio. Ibid., pp. 10–11.

Page 52: "I [have] been . . . never be here." An African American from Louisiana, quoted in Maurice Isserman, *Journey to Freedom: The African-American Great Migration* (New York: Facts on File, 1997), p. 55.

Page 52: "to get [his] family . . . white man's dog." An African American from Greenville, Mississippi, quoted in ibid.

Page 52: "compelled to teach . . . any assistance." An African American from Lexington, Mississippi, quoted in ibid., p. 54.

Page 52: "After twenty years . . . at being civilized." An African American in Chicago, quoted in Litwack, *Trouble in Mind*, p. 490.

Page 53: "The most universal . . . in the courts." A Savannah, Georgia, newspaper, quoted in ibid., p. 561, note 28.

Page 53: On the number of migrants. Josh Sides, *L.A. City Limits: African American Los Angeles from the Great Depression to the Present* (Berkeley: University of California Press, 2003), p. 38.

Page 53: On population in northern cities. Elizabeth Anne Martin, *Detroit and the Great Migration, 1916–1929* (Ann Arbor: Bentley Historical Library, University of Michigan, 1993), p. 3.

Page 55: "There is a difference . . . Alabama you couldn't." Rebecca Stone, quoted in Ezekiel, *Voices from the Corner*, p. 70.

Page 55: "I was made . . . Sam and Bill." An African American in Chicago, quoted in Isserman, *Journey to Freedom*, p. 52.

Page 55: "You'd be astonished . . . It is fearful." Clarisa Sledge, quoted in Litwack, *Trouble in Mind*, p. 488.

Page 55: "You had basically . . . in the Black community." NVLP interview with Asa Hilliard, 2004, transcript pp. 4–5.

Page 56: "all marriages of white . . . or Malaya[ns]." "Jim Crow Laws: Wyoming," History of Jim Crow, http://www.jimcrowhistory.org/scripts/jimcrow/lawsoutside.cgi?state=Wyoming (accessed April 13, 2010).

Page 57: "separate and distinct . . . 25 miles apart." "Jim Crow Laws: Kentucky," History of Jim Crow, http://www.jimcrowhistory.org/scripts/jimcrow/insidesouth.cgi?state=Kentucky (accessed April 13, 2010).

Page 57: "to have Indian . . . of the two races." "Jim Crow Laws: North Dakota," History of Jim Crow, http://www.jimcrowhistory.org/scripts/jimcrow/lawsoutside.cgi?state=North%20Dakota (accessed April 13, 2010).

Page 57: On Indiana state law. Davison M. Douglas, *Jim Crow Moves North: The Battle over Northern School Segregation, 1865–1954* (New York: Cambridge University Press, 2005), p. 5.

Page 57: On Chester, Pennsylvania, schools. Ibid., p. 142.

Page 57: On Hillburn, New York, schools. Sugrue, *Sweet Land of Liberty*, pp. 164–168.

Page 58: "I was the only . . . happens in Pennsylvania too." Interview with Edward Temple, October 16, 2002, National Visionary Leadership Project, housed in the Library of Congress American Folklife Center. NVLP transcript file Temple_Edward.doc, p. 5. Used with permission of the NVLP.

Page 59: "I'd just entered . . . around the radio stations." Interview with Joe Adams, June 11, 2003, National Visionary Leadership Project, housed in the Library of Congress American Folklife Center. NVLP transcript file Adams_Joe_4loc.doc, p. 12. Used with permission of the NVLP.

Page 60: "beginning to have . . . and no training." *Detroit Free Press*, quoted in Martin, *Detroit and the Great Migration*, p. 7.

Page 60: "the Negro comes up . . . to join unions." James Weldon Johnson, quoted in *Black Workers: A Documentary History from Colonial Times to the Present*, eds. Philip S. Foner and Ronald L. Lewis (Philadelphia: Temple University Press, 1989), p. 353.

Page 62: "Me an a white man . . . get back." Bill Broonzy, quoted in Alan Lomax, *The Land Where Blues Began* (New York: New Press, 2002), pp. 442–43.

Page 62: "On receiving jobs . . . operate the machine." Bill Smedley, quoted in *Black Workers*, eds. Foner and Lewis, pp. 385–86.

Page 64: On unemployment figures. Joe William Trotter Jr., *From a Raw Deal to a New Deal? African Americans, 1929–1945* (New York: Oxford University Press, 1996), p. 25.

Page 64: On Urban League unemployment figures. *Black Workers*, eds. Foner and Lewis, p. 35.

Page 65: "I regret to say . . . of the Caucasian race." A factory manager, quoted in Sides, *L.A. City Limits*, p. 82.

Page 65: "It was not uncommon . . . talks and lectures." Charlotta Bass, quoted in Douglas Flamming, *Bound for Freedom: Black Los Angeles in Jim Crow America* (Berkeley: University of California Press, 2005), p. 116.

Page 65: "I consider it . . . get some food." Clayton Russell, quoted in Sides, *L.A. City Limits*, p. 33.

Page 66: "had come . . . with ready cash." A Los Angeles resident, quoted in Flamming, *Bound for Freedom*, p. 51.

Page 66: "Twelve prominent citizens . . . got to get out." Ibid., p. 67.

Page 67: "that no part . . . of Negro blood." Seattle restrictive housing covenant, "Jim Crow Laws: Washington," History of Jim Crow, http://www.jimcrowhistory.org/scripts/jimcrow/lawsoutside.cgi?state=Washington (accessed April 13, 2010).

Page 69: "WE WANT WHITE . . . COMMUNITY." Sugrue, *Sweet Land of Liberty*, pp. 67–68.

Page 69: "through large derelict . . . in her backyard." Rachel Robinson, quoted in Rachel Robinson with Lee Daniels, *Jackie Robinson: An Intimate Portrait* (New York: Abrams, 1996), p. 130.

Page 70: "'There isn't any . . . colored,' she said." Madison Jones, quoted in Alexander L. Crosby, *In These 10 Cities: Discrimination in Housing* (New York: Public Affairs Committee, 1951), pp. 26–28.

Page 70: "We didn't put the lights . . . riot car screaming." Mrs. Roscoe Johnson, quoted in ibid., p. 18.

Page 71: "A race without . . . but strength." Marcus Garvey, quoted in James R. Grossman, *A Chance to Make Good: African Americans, 1900–1929* (New York: Oxford University Press, 1997), p. 143.

Page 72: "every Sunday . . . of Black women." Interview with Elma Lewis, December 17, 2002, National Visionary Leadership Project, housed in the Library of Congress American Folklife Center. NVLP transcript file Lewis_Elma.doc, p. 4. Used with permission of the NVLP.

Page 72: "wonderful . . . wanted to be." Interview with Norma Miller, June 1, 2006, National Visionary Leadership Project, housed in the Library of Congress American Folklife Center. NVLP transcript file Miller_Norma.doc, pp. 15, 21. Used with permission of the NVLP.

Page 74: On the East St. Louis protest march. Grossman, *A Chance to Make Good*, p. 127.

Page 78: On segregation during the Wilson administration. Nicholas Patler, *Jim Crow and the Wilson Administration: Protesting Federal Segregation in the Early Twentieth Century* (Boulder: University of Colorado Press, 2004).

Page 79: "the friction . . . thereby be removed." Woodrow Wilson, quoted in Kathleen L. Wolgemuth, "Woodrow Wilson and Federal Segregation," *The Journal of Negro History*, vol. 44., no. 2 (April 1959), p. 163, http://www.jstor.org/stable/2716036 (accessed December 21, 2010).

Page 79: On African Americans soldiers. David M. Kennedy, *Over Here: The First World War and American Society* (New York: Oxford University Press, 1982), pp. 160, 161.

Page 80: "the mass of . . . labor battalions." U.S. Army report, quoted in ibid., p. 162.

Page 80: On black American soldiers in France. Ibid., p. 199.

Page 80: "though we carried . . . of the procession." Ellen Tarry, quoted in Grossman, *A Chance to Make Good*, p. 133.

Page 80: "I had a nice . . . down *these* streets." Bill Broonzy, quoted in Lomax, *Land Where Blues Began*, p. 435.

Page 82: On the post–World War I North. Kennedy, *Over Here*, pp. 279–83.

Page 82: On African Americans and federal government programs. Sugrue, *Sweet Land of Liberty*, pp. 51–53.

Page 83: "to remain . . . resigning." Eleanor Roosevelt quoted in Angelina Keating, *Eleanor Roosevelt* (San Francisco: Pomegranate Communications, 2006), p. 33.

Page 84: On black workers in the aircraft industry. Paula F. Pfeffer, *A. Philip Randolph, Pioneer of the Civil Rights Movement* (Baton Rouge: Louisiana State University Press, 1990), p. 46.

Page 84: "I suggest that . . . WITH GLOVES OFF." A. Philip Randolph, quoted in Jervis Anderson, *A. Philip Randolph: A Biographical Portrait* (Berkeley: University of California Press, 1986), p. 249.

Page 86: "Waiting in line . . . for n_____s." Pearl W. Mack Jr., Library of Congress Veterans History Project, http://lcweb2.loc.gov/diglib/vhp-stories/loc.natlib.afc2001001.05764/pageturner?ID=pm00001001&page=2 (accessed January 10, 2011).

Page 86: "Whenever one of us . . . command the units." Isaiah A. McCoy Jr. interview, Library of Congress Veterans History Project, http://lcweb2.loc.gov/diglib/vhp-stories/loc.natlib.afc2001001.02503/ (accessed January 10, 2011).

Page 87: "I had made a decision . . . that said, 'Colored.'" Interview with Lee Archer, March 12, 2002, National Visionary Leadership Project, housed in the Library of Congress American Folklife Center. NVLP transcript file Archer_Lee_loc.doc., pp. 13, 21. Used with permission of the NVLP.

Page 89: On Tuskegee airmen citations. *The African American Odyssey*, Debra Newman Ham, ed. (Washington, D.C.: Library of Congress, 1998), p. 103.

Page 89: On black pilots' awards. Trotter, *From a Raw Deal to a New Deal?* p. 95.

Page 90: "democratic rights . . . during the war." A. Philip Randolph, quoted in Pfeffer, *A. Philip Randolph*, p. 51.

Page 90: "kept a running . . . truckful of . . . GOT TO GO!" Pauli Murray, quoted in Sugrue, *Sweet Land of Liberty*, p. 74.

Page 90: "DOWN WITH DISCRIMINATION" . . . "COLOR BLIND." Ibid., p. 75.

Page 91: "Destroy segregation." James Farmer, quoted in *African American Lives*, eds. Henry Louis Gates Jr. and Evelyn Brooks Higginbotham (New York: Oxford University Press, 2004), p. 287.

Page 92: "all you had . . . qualified for a job." Juanita Nelson, quoted in Sugrue, *Sweet Land of Liberty*, p. 135.

Page 92: On the 1943 racial riots. Litwack, *How Free Is Free?* p. 84.

Page 93: "VICTORY DEMANDS . . . REAR TO FRONT." Ibid., p. 78.

Page 95: "Every stadium . . . in the mail." Robinson, *Jackie Robinson*, pp. 70, 72.

Page 96: "JUST SAW . . . AND A GENTLEMAN." Telegram, quoted in Harry Katz et al., *Baseball Americana: Treasures from the Library of Congress* (New York: HarperCollins, 2009), p. 213.

Page 96: "Each day we would . . . blacks was wrong." Igal Roodenko interview, Documenting the American South oral history project, University of North Carolina, http://docsouth.unc.edu/sohp/B-0010/B-0010.html (accessed November 10, 2010).

Page 100: On *Brown v. Board of Education*. See the Brown Foundation, http://brownvboard.org/content/background-overview-summary (accessed December 21, 2010); National Archives, http://www.archives.gov/education/lessons/brown-v-board/bios.html (accessed November 15, 2010); Juan Williams, *Eyes on the Prize: America's Civil Rights Years, 1954–1965* (New York: Penguin, 1988).

Page 100: "take [their] names off . . . with the petition." Liza Briggs, quoted in Williams, *Eyes on the Prize*, pp. 19–20.

Page 102: "the school . . . had to come." Joan Johns Cobb, quoted at the Congress of Racial Equality, http://www.core-online.org/History/barbara_johns1.htm (accessed September 23, 2010).

Page 104: "segregation of white . . . believe that it does." Brown decision quoted at FindLaw, http://laws.findlaw.com/us/347/483.html (accessed January 10, 2011).

Page 104: "a new birth of freedom." *Washington Post*, quoted in Williams, *Eyes on the Prize*, p. 35.

Page 105: "Where a State . . . on equal terms." Brown decision quoted at FindLaw, http://laws.findlaw.com/us/347/483.html (accessed January 10, 2011).

BIBLIOGRAPHY

* Indicates books suitable for children

Anderson, Jervis. *A. Philip Randolph: A Biographical Portrait.* Berkeley: University of California Press, 1986. (First published in 1972.)

*Bair, Barbara. *Though Justice Sleeps: African Americans, 1880–1900.* New York: Oxford University Press, 1997. (Series: Kelley, Robin D. G., and Earl Lewis, eds. *The Young Oxford History of African Americans.* New York: Oxford University Press, 1995–97.)

*Bolden, Tonya. *Tell All the Children Our Story: Memories and Mementos of Being Young and Black in America.* New York: Abrams, 2001.

Brown, Nikki L. M., and Barry M. Stentiford, eds. *The Jim Crow Encyclopedia.* 2 vols. Westport, CT: Greenwood Press, 2008.

Chafe, William H., Raymond Gavins, and Robert Korstad, eds. *Remembering Jim Crow: African Americans Tell About Life in the Segregated South.* New York: New Press, 2001.

Crosby, Alexander L. *In These 10 Cities: Discrimination in Housing.* New York: Public Affairs Committee, 1951.

Dailey, Jane, ed. *The Age of Jim Crow.* New York: W. W. Norton, 2009.

Douglas, Davison M. *Jim Crow Moves North: The Battle over Northern School Segregation, 1865–1954.* New York: Cambridge University Press, 2005.

Egerton, John. *Speak Now Against the Day: The Generation Before the Civil Rights Movement in the South.* New York: Knopf, 1994.

Ezekiel, Raphael S. *Voices from the Corner: Poverty and Racism in the Inner City.* Philadelphia: Temple University Press, 1984.

Flamming, Douglas. *Bound for Freedom: Black Los Angeles in Jim Crow America.* Berkeley: University of California Press, 2005.

Foner, Philip S., and Ronald L. Lewis, eds. *Black Workers: A Documentary History from Colonial Times to the Present.* Philadelphia: Temple University Press, 1989.

Franklin, Buck Colbert. *My Life and an Era: The Autobiography of Buck Colbert Franklin.* John Hope Franklin and John Whittington Franklin, eds. Baton Rouge: Louisiana State University Press, 1997.

Franklin, John Hope. *Mirror to America: The Autobiography of John Hope Franklin.* New York: Farrar, Straus and Giroux, 2005.

Garfinkel, Herbert. *When Negroes March: The March on Washington Movement in the Organizational Politics for FEPC.* Glencoe, IL: Free Press, 1949.

Gates, Henry Louis Jr., and Evelyn Brooks Higginbotham, eds. *African American Lives.* New York: Oxford University Press, 2004.

Grimshaw, Allen D., ed. *A Social History of Racial Violence.* New Brunswick, NJ: Aldine Transaction, 2009. (First published in 1969.)

*Grossman, James R. *A Chance to Make Good: African Americans 1900–1929.* New York: Oxford University Press, 1997. (Series: Kelley, Robin D. G., and Earl Lewis, eds. *The Young Oxford History of African Americans.* New York: Oxford University Press, 1995–97.)

Ham, Debra Newman, ed. *The African American Odyssey: An Exhibition at the Library of Congress.* Washington, DC: Library of Congress, 1998.

Hornsby, Alton, Jr. *Chronology of African American History: From 1492 to the Present.* 2nd ed. Detroit: Gale Research, 1997.

*Isserman, Maurice. *Journey to Freedom: The African-American Great Migration.* New York: Facts on File, 1997.

Katz, Harry, et. al. *Baseball Americana: Treasures from the Library of Congress.* New York: HarperCollins, 2009.

Keating, Anjelina Michelle. *Eleanor Roosevelt.* San Francisco: Pomegranate Communications, 2006.

Kennedy, David M. *Over Here: The First World War and American Society.* New York: Oxford University Press, 1982. (First published in 1980.)

*King, Casey, and Linda Barrett Osborne. *Oh, Freedom! Kids Talk About the Civil Rights Movement with the People Who Made It Happen.* New York: Knopf, 1997.

Lemann, Nicholas. *The Promised Land: The Great Black Migration and How It Changed America.* New York: Knopf, 1991.

Lewis, Catherine M., and J. Richard Lewis, eds. *Jim Crow America: A Documentary History.* Fayetteville: University of Arkansas Press, 2009.

Library of Congress. *A Small Nation of People: W. E. B. Du Bois and African American Portraits of Progress.* New York: Amistad, 2003.

Litwack, Leon F. *How Free Is Free? The Long Death of Jim Crow.* Cambridge, MA: Harvard University Press, 2009.

———. *Trouble in Mind: Black Southerners in the Age of Jim Crow.* New York: Knopf, 1998.

Lomax, Alan. *The Land Where Blues Began.* New York: New Press, 2002. (First published in 1993.)

Martin, Elizabeth Anne. *Detroit and the Great Migration, 1916–1929.* Ann Arbor: Bentley Historical Library, University of Michigan, 1993. (*Bentley Historical Library Bulletin* no. 40, January 1993.)

Medley, Keith Weldon. *We As Freemen: Plessy v. Ferguson.* Gretna, LA: Pelican Publishing, 2003.

*Meltzer, Milton and August Meier. *Time of Trial, Time of Hope: The Negro in America, 1919–1941.* Garden City, NY: Doubleday, 1966.

Murray, Pauli. *Pauli Murray: The Autobiography of a Black Activist, Feminist, Lawyer, Priest, and Poet.* Knoxville: University of Tennessee Press, 1989.

———. *Proud Shoes: The Story of an American Family.* Boston: Beacon Press, 1999. (First published in 1956.)

The Negro Motorist Green Book. Victor H. Green, ed. Published yearly 1936–64 by Victor H. Green and Co., Leonia, NJ.

Newman, Edwin S. *The Law of Civil Rights and Civil Liberties.* New York: Oceana Publications, 1949.

*Osborne, Linda Barrett. *Traveling the Freedom Road: From Slavery and the Civil War Through Reconstruction.* New York: Abrams Books for Young Readers/Washington, DC: Library of Congress, 2009.

Patler, Nicholas. *Jim Crow and the Wilson Administration: Protesting Federal Segregation in the Early Twentieth Century.* Boulder: University Press of Colorado, 2004.

Pfeffer, Paula F. *A. Philip Randolph, Pioneer of the Civil Rights Movement.* Baton Rouge: Louisiana State University Press, 1990.

Rittenhouse, Jennifer. *Growing Up Jim Crow: How Black and White Southern Children Learned Race.* Chapel Hill: University of North Carolina Press, 2006.

Robinson, Rachel, with Lee Daniels. *Jackie Robinson: An Intimate Portrait.* New York: Abrams, 1996.

Sides, Josh. *L.A. City Limits: African American Los Angeles from the Great Depression to the Present.* Berkeley: University of California Press, 2003.

Sugrue, Thomas J. *Sweet Land of Liberty: The Forgotten Struggle for Civil Rights in the North.* New York: Random House, 2008.

*Trotter, Joe William, Jr. *From a Raw Deal to a New Deal? African Americans, 1929–1945.* New York: Oxford University Press, 1996. (Series: Kelley, Robin D. G., and Earl Lewis, eds. *The Young Oxford History of African Americans.* New York: Oxford University Press, 1995–97.)

Wilkerson, Isabel. *The Warmth of Other Suns.* New York: Random House, 2010.

Williams, Juan. *Eyes on the Prize: America's Civil Rights Years, 1954–1965.* New York: Penguin Books, 1988. (First published in 1987.)

Woodward, C. Vann. *Origins of the New South, 1877–1913.* Baton Rouge: Louisiana State University Press, 1951.

———. *The Strange Career of Jim Crow.* New York: Oxford University Press, 2002. (First published in 1955.)

A NOTE ON SOURCES

The Library of Congress is a rich source for materials on segregation and the quest for civil rights. It includes the archives of the National Association for the Advancement of Colored People (NAACP); interviews in the Veterans History Project of the American Folklife Center; early photographs of segregated schools and communities by noted photographers including Lewis Hine and Frances Benjamin Johnston; and the incomparable photos in the Farm Security Administration–Office of War Information collection in the Prints and Photographs Division, in which photographers such as Gordon Parks, Marion Post Wolcott, Jack Delano, and Dorothea Lange documented American life during the Great Depression and the years of World War II. The Library's American Folklife Center houses tapes and transcripts from the National Visionary Leadership Project, a collection of interviews with African American elders begun in 2001. This primary source material is accessible on the NVLP Web site, www.visionaryproject.org, and is permanently archived at the Library of Congress. I have also used interviews from the Behind the Veil Project, housed at the Center for Documentary Studies at Duke University; and the Southern Oral History Program, based at the University of North Carolina, Chapel Hill.

IMAGE CREDITS

Picture frame images on the following pages are copyright © 2010 www.free-photo-frames.com: vi, x, 50, 76
Page 54: "Our Own Community Grocery Store and Delicatessen" (ca. 1940). © Aaron Siskind Foundation. Used with permission.
Page 70: Untitled (1950). Photograph by Marion Palfi. © 1998 Arizona Board of Regents, Center for Creative Photography.
Page 71: "Garvey Militia" (1924). © Donna Mussenden VanDerZee. Used with permission.
Page 73 (left): "Couple in Raccoon Coats" (1932). © Donna Mussenden VanDerZee. Used with permission.

All of the images in *Miles to Go for Freedom* can be found in the collections of the Library of Congress. Only images from the Prints and Photographs Division have negative numbers, which are indicated below. To order digital or print reproductions of images (with some restrictions) that are accompanied by a Library of Congress negative number (e.g., LC-USZ62-XXXXX; LC-USZC4-XXXXX; LC-DIG-ppmsca-XXXXX), contact the Library of Congress Duplication Services, Washington, DC 20540-4570. Telephone: (202)707-5640; fax: (202)707-1771; e-mail: duplicationservices@loc.gov. Visit the Duplication Services Web site at http://www.loc.gov/preserv/pds for further information.

Key: Prints and Photographs Division = P&P; Manuscript Division = MSS; General Collections = GC

FRONTISPIECE
(Also on front cover) P&P, LC-USZC2-5399

PREFACE
Page vi: P&P, LC-USZ62-124866

INTRODUCTION
Page x: P&P, LC-DIG-ppmsc-00216
Page 2 (top): GC
Page 2 (bottom): P&P, LC-USZ62-129840
Page 5: P&P, LC-USZ62-116926
Page 6: P&P, LC-USZC4-4658
Page 8: P&P, LC-USZ62-19234
Page 10 and front cover: P&P, LC-USZ62-124686
Page 13 and back cover: P&P, LC-DIG-pga-01619

THE SOUTH
Page 14: P&P, LC-USZ62-135594
Page 17: P&P, LC-USZ62-104541
Page 19: P&P, LC-USZ62-115416
Page 20: P&P, LC-USZ62-129093
Page 21: P&P, LC-USZ62-37348
Page 23: P&P, LC-USZ62-33786
Pages 24–5 and front cover: P&P, LC-USZ62-119522
Page 26: P&P, LC-USZ62-112455
Page 28: P&P, LC-USF34-035087-D
Page 30 (top): P&P, LC-USZ62-99294
Page 30 (bottom): P&P, LC-USZ62-99293
Page 31: P&P, LC-USZ62-120752
Page 33: P&P, LC-USZ62-118226
Page 35 (top): P&P, LC-USZ62-35750

Page 35 (bottom): P&P, LC-USZ62-38625
Page 36: P&P, LC-USF34-017295-C
Page 37: P&P, LC-USZ62-117125
Page 39: P&P, LC-USZ62-49479
Page 40: P&P, LC-USZ62-51555
Page 41: P&P, LC-USZ62-124911
Page 42: P&P, LC-USZ62-107755
Page 44 (left): GC
Page 44 (right): GC
Page 45: P&P, LC-USZ62-130357
Page 46: P&P, LC-USZ62-33788
Page 48: P&P, LC-USZ62-84483
Page 49 and front cover: P&P, LC-DIG-ppmsca-00388

THE NORTH
Page 50 and front cover: P&P, LC-DIG-ppmsc-00256
Page 52: P&P, LC-USF34-040841-D
Page 53: P&P, LC-DIG-nclc-04050
Page 54: P&P, LC-USZC4-4737
Page 56: P&P, LC-USZ62-107951
Page 58: P&P, LC-DIG-ppmsca-10436
Page 59: P&P, LC-USZ62-33785
Page 61: P&P, LC-USZ62-46395
Page 62: P&P, LC-USZ62-130701
Page 63: P&P, LC-USZC4-2766
Page 64: P&P, LC-USZ62-43454
Page 66: P&P, LC-USW38-000138-D
Page 67: P&P, LC-USZ62-124239
Page 68 (top): P&P, LC-USW3-016549-C
Page 68 (bottom): P&P, LC-USW3-016547-C
Page 70: P&P, LC-USZ62-130664
Page 71: P&P, LC-USZ62-117062

Page 73 (left): P&P, LC-USZ62-83361
Page 73 (right): P&P, LC-USZ62-123107
Page 74: P&P, LC-USZC4-11580
Page 75 (top): P&P, LC-USZ62-33789
Page 75 (bottom): P&P, LC-USZ62-110581

THE NATION
Page 76: MSS
Page 78: GC
Page 80: P&P, LC-USZ62-116442
Page 81: P&P, LC-USZ62-110591
Page 83 and back cover: P&P, LC-USZ62-116730
Page 85 (left): P&P, LC-USF34-063103-D
Page 85 (right): P&P, LC-USW3-034282-C
Page 87 (left): P&P, LC-DIG-ppmsca-13269
Page 87 (right): P&P, LC-USZ62-35361
Page 88 (top): P&P, LC-USZ62-58098
Page 88 (bottom): P&P, LC-USZ62-94040
Page 91 and back flap: P&P, LC-USW3-T01-037968-E
Page 92: P&P, LC-USW3-011400-C
Page 93: P&P, LC-USZ62-132815
Page 94 and front cover: MSS
Page 97: P&P, LC-USZ62-138414
Page 98: P&P, LC-USZ62-61026
Page 99: P&P, LC-USZ62-84502
Page 101 (top): P&P, LC-USZ61-2156
Page 101 (bottom): P&P, LC-DIG-ppmsca-05512
Page 103: P&P, LC-USZ62-112704
Page 105: P&P, LC-USZ62-113496
Page 106: P&P, LC-USZ62-134572
Page 107: P&P, LC-DIG-ppmsca-03119

ACKNOWLEDGMENTS

Making a book is a collaborative effort. I am lucky to work with two excellent teams, one at the Library of Congress, the other at Abrams. Thanks to Ralph Eubanks, Director of the Library of Congress Publishing Office, for his continued support for my work and for our many conversations that illuminate African American history for me. Thanks, too, to Howard Reeves, my editor at Abrams, who has a fine eye for clarity, the patience to get things right, and the enthusiasm to keep me going.

I am grateful to the writers, editors, and staff of the Publishing Office for their unflagging encouragement: Aimee Hess, Blaine Marshall, Susan Reyburn, Myint Myint San, Peggy Wagner, and Athena Angelos. Special thanks to Hicks Wogan for his skill in photo research and his apt suggestions. At Abrams, I appreciate the help of managing editor James Armstrong, editorial assistant Jenna Pocius, and copy editor Maureen Klier. Designer Maria T. Middleton has a gift for creating a visually stunning design that complements the text and illustrations.

Thanks to Jeff Bridgers, Jan Grenci, Marilyn Ibach, and Barbara Natanson of the Prints and Photographs Division; Judith Gray, Ann Hoog, Guha Shankar, and Kate Stewart of the American Folklife Center; and other staff of the Library who assisted me with research. Paul Hogroian of Duplication Services was very helpful in obtaining copies of images. Keith Weldon Medley, author of *We As Freemen: Plessy v. Ferguson*, was generous with advice on finding an image of Homer Plessy. (There is none.) Thanks also to Casey King, who brought me on as coauthor of *Oh, Freedom!* and started me on the path to thinking and writing about civil rights and segregation.

Special thanks go to the National Visionary Leadership Project (NVLP), a nonprofit educational organization that chronicles the lives of accomplished African American elders to unite the generations and create a blueprint for the leaders of tomorrow. The NVLP records, preserves, and distributes through various media the wisdom of extraordinary African Americans who have shaped American history. Cheryl S. Clarke of the NVLP provided invaluable assistance in tracking down rights to the interviews from the project.

As always, I want to thank my husband, Bob, and my daughter, Catherine, who never tire of sharing ideas, commenting on drafts, and keeping me on track; and offer many thanks to my son, Nick, a graduate student in American history, whose knowledge has helped me to write about a complex subject with accuracy and attention to nuance, and to share with a young audience our love of history.

INDEX